Longing For A Breakthrough

Jonathan Winchell

Copyright © 2025

All Rights Reserved

ISBN:

Contents

About the Author iii

Introduction: Through My Eyes v

Chapter 1: Beginnings and Belongings 1

Chapter 2: Discovering Strengths and Seeking Independence 6

Chapter 3: The Family Business and Finding Purpose 12

Chapter 4: Health, Wellness, and Self-Care 17

Chapter 5: Seeking Support and Connections Outside Family .. 24

Chapter 6: Exploring Passions and Hobbies 34

Chapter 7: The Emotional Impact of Disability 44

Chapter 8: Struggles with Mobility and Accessibility 48

Chapter 9: Forgiveness, Acceptance, and Moving Forward 53

Chapter 10: Interaction with my siblings 57

Chapter 11: Empowering My Independence 68

Chapter 12: My Future Plans 81

About the Author

My name is Jonathan Winchell, and most of my favorite memories are of being with the family, going to Disneyland, and being on rides. I even remember that, in kindergarten, before going to bed, I watched The Wonderful World of Disney in 1971. The Wonderful World of Disney aired from 1969 to 1979 on Sundays at 7:00 pm on NBC. I still watch old cartoons, share my history and knowledge with my sons and wife, treasure my Disney memorabilia, and display my lunch boxes. I always enjoyed watching Disney movies from the 1900s through the 1970s. My favorite moments were going to the Lafayette Park Theatre in my hometown of Lafayette, California, in 1977, watching Saturday Night Fever starring John Travolta. I even worked at the Lafayette Park Theatre in the 90s. I also volunteered at the Orinda Theatre, where I worked at the box office, served concessions and I was a volunteer of the year in 2023 where my family and friends were very proud of me. I also used to work at the Veranda Luxe Theatre in Concord, California where I worked at the box office, I also received my food handlers certificate which I completed on my first try and my alcoholic Beverage Control license. I have also been very supportive and sponsored non profit organizations for various communities in different cities near my area from 2000 to present.I have a Facebook page, FilmBlogsAreUs, where I review films of all genres. I am also a published author. My Autobiography, Being Different Than My Family: Living With Mosaic Down Syndrome Chromosome #21, highlights my experience with this rare condition, which affects less than 1% of people with Mosaic Down Syndrome.

Page Blank Intentionally

Introduction: Through My Eyes

It's hard to explain growing up feeling like an extra piece of a puzzle. I was the same as everyone else, but then again, I wasn't. I've always known I'm different, and that difference seemed to stick to me like a shadow. My family has always told me, "You're just like anyone else," and yet, I could see it in their eyes, in the way they talked to me, in the way they made decisions for me. There was this subtle shift, this protective barrier as if they were shielding me from a world they thought I couldn't handle.

I don't know if anyone else has this feeling—that sense of living behind a pane of glass. For me, it's like watching the world carry on around me, seeing life happen, but somehow, I'm not a part of it. People see me. They say my name, smile at me, talk with me, and sometimes even laugh at my jokes, but still, that feeling stays with me, this strange loneliness that's hard to explain. Maybe that's why I've always felt so different, so separate.

I was born with mosaic Down syndrome, which sounds like a fancy way of saying I've had a lot of extra challenges in life. But that's not how I see it—not really. To me, this is just who I am. It's my world, my experience, and maybe because it's all I've known, it doesn't always feel like a disadvantage. At least, not until I look around and notice how others seem to feel about me, the way they try to fit me into their ideas of who they think I should be. It's a strange feeling knowing you're loved but not quite accepted for who you really are.

My family says, "Jonathan, we don't see you any differently." They say, "We're so proud of you, Jonathan." And yet, I know they're not really hearing me. I can feel it. It's in the small things, the way they make decisions for me without asking, the way they worry about me so much that they don't realize how much it holds me back. They call it love, but it feels more like a cage—a beautiful, well-meaning, but confining cage.

When I was young, I didn't understand what it meant to have mosaic Down syndrome. I only knew that there were things people didn't think I could do. There was a look they'd give me—first my parents, then my teachers, even my siblings—like they were silently reminding me of my limits, like they didn't trust me to handle much on my own. I used to lie awake at night, thinking, *"Why don't they believe in me?"* It's a question that still haunts me.

The hardest part is wanting so badly to belong but feeling like you're on the outside, looking in. I've been blessed in so many ways; I know that. I have a family, a roof over my head, friends I can laugh with, and stories to tell. But there's a hollowness in that gratitude because I've spent my life feeling like a burden, someone they had to accommodate rather than someone they could truly see.

I remember my father, his quiet way of holding the world together, his silent strength. He was a man of few words, and in my younger years, I admired him deeply. He provided for us, built a family business, and set everything up so that his children would have stability and purpose. But with me, it always felt different. I think he wanted to understand me, but maybe he never could. He'd watch me when I talked about my dreams or when I asked questions he didn't have the answers to, and sometimes, I'd see him frown, like he wasn't sure what to make of me.

When he passed away in 2007, everything changed. It was like a storm ripped through our family, leaving us scattered and silent, each of us retreating into ourselves. My siblings grew distant, absorbed in their own lives. My mother tried her best, but I could feel her worry intensify, her protectiveness settling over me like a shadow. They say they want the best for me and that they see me as independent, but their actions tell another story. They tell me to be myself, but only if it's the version of "myself" they approve of, the version that's safe and easy to manage.

The truth is, I want to live my own life and make my own choices, even if I fall along the way. But they don't understand that. They don't see that my soul longs to stretch beyond the safety nets they've put around me. I'm not saying I don't need help sometimes; we all do. But I need to be allowed to stand on my own, to feel the weight of my own life in my hands.

There were so many nights when I'd sit alone, watching the lights from outside my window and wondering what life would be like if I could step outside of everyone else's expectations for me. I would daydream about things I'd never share—running my own business, traveling somewhere new, making a real difference somehow. I dreamed of being someone strong and fearless, someone people could depend on. But as time went on, I stopped talking about my dreams. My family would just pat my shoulder and say, "That's nice, Jonathan." They didn't understand. They couldn't see how badly I needed them to say, "You can do it. We believe in you."

In a way, I don't blame them. They think they're doing what's best. But I wish they could understand that what they see as love sometimes feels like confinement. Their good intentions build walls around me, keeping me safe, yes, but also keeping me from becoming all I can be.

I'm still learning what it means to be me, but I know one thing for sure: I'm not just my disability. I'm more than the limits they see. I'm a person with a mind full of ideas, a heart full of love, and a spirit that's always fighting to break free. Maybe, one day, they'll see me for who I am, not just who they want me to be.

This is my story, told my way. It's not perfect, but it's real. And in the end, maybe that's all any of us can ask for.

Longing For A Breakthrough

Chapter 1: Beginnings and Belongings

From a young age, I sensed that people saw me differently. They'd say I had a "unique spirit," something that made me stand out. But sometimes, standing out felt more like standing apart, a kind of distance I didn't always understand. I felt like I was on a stage, with others watching, expecting me to act a certain way. I came to realize that my mosaic Down syndrome shaped how others saw me, and over time, it began to shape how I saw myself. As I grew, I learned that others' perceptions could influence how I felt about myself, but I didn't want to be held back by anyone's expectations.

Growing up, my parents were my first allies, my protectors, and my guides in a world that didn't always make space for me. They'd often remind me, "Jonathan, you're just as capable as anyone else. Your path may look different, but that doesn't make it any less valuable." And while I appreciated their support, there were moments when I wished they'd let me explore on my own, even if that meant making mistakes. It's hard to learn who you are when the people around you are so focused on keeping you safe. But I understood where they were coming from—they wanted to see me happy, not hurt or disheartened.

One particular memory I have is of a day in Junior High school. I wanted to play tennis with other students, and I was determined to do well. I wanted to show everyone that I could be just as quick and strong as they were. However, prior to playing I needed to get my parents approval to play at Junior High school, and that is when they hired a private instructor for me at my parents' house. I never had the chance to play tennis in Junior High School, and my family gave me looks of hesitation mixed with caution, as if they were worried I'd get hurt. I felt a pang of frustration, but I didn't let it stop me. It was during summer camp that I was traveling to a tennis camp where I played my hardest and had a great time. Unfortunately, looking back, I really wanted to play tennis with my classmates and improve my skills in throwing the ball up with all my strength.

At the end of the summer camp, my family patted me on the back and said, "Good job, Jonathan! You did better than I expected." They meant it as a compliment, but it stung. It was a reminder that people saw me differently and that they measured my success by a different standard. In their eyes, my victories were small, just pleasant surprises rather than achievements I'd worked for. I felt pride in my effort, but the shadow of their lowered expectations was something I couldn't easily shake.

I began to understand that my journey would be one of proving myself—not only to others but to myself as well. I realized that the world had certain ideas about what someone like me could or couldn't do and that those ideas didn't match the dreams I had for myself. It was a hard truth to accept, but it became fuel for my determination. I chose not to let it defeat me. Instead, I decided to use it as motivation to work twice as hard to meet the standards I set for myself rather than the ones others imposed on me.

In high school, I started to explore more of the world beyond my family's watchful eyes. I wanted to know what it felt like to make decisions independently, to experience life without a constant safety net. My parents were supportive, but I could tell they were nervous. They'd spent so many years sheltering me, guiding me, making sure I didn't face unnecessary challenges. But I knew that to grow, I needed to find my way, even if it meant taking risks or making mistakes.

Longing For A Breakthrough

One of the first steps I took toward independence was finding a job. My father ran a small family business, and I thought it would be a good place to start. I knew the work might be simple, but it was a chance to prove myself and show that I could contribute meaningfully. I wished my dad had welcomed me with open arms, giving me tasks that were manageable yet impactful; however, I learned how to organize the files, learned the basics of customer service, and eventually handled small parts of daily operations on my own. I was the one who took on more responsibility, not my dad. It was my Dad who trusted everyone to take on more responsibility, and I eventually took on every task that I completed.

Working at the family business taught me a lot about responsibility. It wasn't just about showing up and doing the tasks—I learned the importance of consistency, of making a commitment and sticking to it. I realized that my contributions, no matter how small, mattered. Each day I showed up, I felt a little more capable and a little more confident in my abilities. I did not have anyone watch over me; I knew that the effort I put in was on my own.

There was one day at work that stood out. I was helping a prospective tenant who wanted an apartment that seemed very nice, checking in to see if he liked the apartment and what he needed. I could feel he was very satisfied. Years later, I found out that he was a secret shopper, and my family had a mixture of impatience and doubt. They mentioned to me that it was supposed to be for the other manager on staff and not me. But instead of letting my family's attitude rattle me, I took a deep breath and focused on the task. Eventually, I found what he was looking for, and when he left, I felt a small surge of pride. It was a reminder that I could handle situations on my own, even if they were challenging, according to my family. It felt good to overcome the doubt in my family business and in myself.

Jonathan Winchell

Outside of work, I tried to build my independence in small ways. I started managing my own schedule, planning my day around my responsibilities and my hobbies. I enjoyed sports and took up tennis, a way to clear my mind and set small goals for myself. At first, my mom insisted on playing tennis with me, also worried about my safety. But as I grew more confident, I asked if I could go play tennis with her, explaining that it was important for me to have that time together. Eventually, she would rather pay for me to get private instructions, and that small victory felt like a big step.

These early experiences laid the foundation for my journey toward independence. They taught me that I was capable of more than others sometimes gave me credit for and that my worth was defined by their expectations. I began to see myself in a new light, where I persevered on my own. I did not need constant guidance, but I was someone who could grow, adapt, and thrive in my own way. And with each passing year, I grew more determined to prove to myself and to the world that I was more than my mosaic Down syndrome. I was Jonathan—someone with dreams, a desire to contribute, and a spirit that wouldn't be confined by labels.

One of the most powerful moments that I thought of on my own was sharing and telling my dad about my goals while sitting down with him. I wish my dad had said to me, "Jonathan, you've done an incredible job here at the business. I'm proud of you, but I want you to know that you can do whatever you set your mind to. Don't feel like you're limited to staying here." Hearing those words from my dad would have meant more to me than he could ever know. It was like a door opening, an invitation to dream beyond what I'd ever thought possible.

Longing For A Breakthrough

As I reflect on those early years, I realize that each challenge, each small victory, added up to something much bigger—a foundation of resilience and strength. I learned that my journey might look different but that it was mine to shape. I didn't need to follow anyone else's path or fit into anyone's expectations. I was forging my own way, one step at a time, and that was enough.

This was only the beginning, but I knew that my journey was one worth fighting for. I understood that life would be full of challenges but also full of opportunities to show myself—and the world—that I was more than what they saw. I was Jonathan, ready to take on whatever came my way.

Jonathan Winchell

Chapter 2: Discovering Strengths and Seeking Independence

It's funny, looking back, how something as small as a part-time job felt like a lifeline to me. The theater job wasn't a huge thing to anyone else, but to me, it was a step into a world that wasn't filtered through my family's watchful eyes. It was like my own little island of independence, a place where I could prove to myself, and maybe even to them, that I was capable.

I remember that first day like it was yesterday, and this was in 2018 at the Veranda Luxe Theatre in Concord, Ca. where my hands were shaking as I was giving the right change from the cash register to the movie-goers. I didn't practice because one of the managers was worried about me making mistakes, however it was other employees that made it easy for me. My supervisor, a young guy named Matt with a half-smile and an easygoing way, who had a half-smile and showed me around. He walked me through everything—the popcorn machine, the soda fountain, the ticket scanner. I did not feel overwhelmed because, in the 1990s, I worked at a different theater in my hometown, the Lafayette Park Theatre, but I kept nodding, trying to absorb it all.

"Don't worry," Matt said with a grin when he saw my worried expression. "You'll get the hang of it. Everyone messes up on their first day."

I don't know if he was just trying to make me feel better, but his words stuck with me. Everyone messes up. It wasn't a crime. It wasn't the end of the world. I took a deep breath, felt the tension in my shoulders loosen just a little, and gave him a smile. That small, simple reassurance from someone outside my family meant more than he could have known. It felt like permission to just be a person, to make mistakes, to be allowed to struggle without someone swooping in to save me.

My first few shifts were tough, tougher than I'd expected. There was so much to remember, so many small details that seemed to pile up faster than I could handle. I'd spill popcorn on the counter, fill cups with too much ice, and forget which button to press on the soda machine. Every time I messed up, I'd feel my cheeks flush, and a small voice in my head would whisper, "See? You're not cut out for this."

But then, just when I thought I couldn't keep up, I'd catch a glimpse of the customers. The way they'd smile when I handed them their drinks, the way they'd thank me with a quick nod like I was part of their experience, part of their night out. I wasn't just a "special case" or someone who needed looking after. In those moments, I was just Jonathan, doing a job and making people happy, even if it was in small ways. And that feeling... that feeling was everything.

One night, after a long shift, Matt clapped me on the back and said, "You did great today, man. You're getting faster." That simple praise meant the world to me. I felt my chest swell with pride, the kind that lingered even as I climbed into the car where my mom was waiting to pick me up. But the moment I sat down, her familiar questions came flooding in.

"How was work, Jonathan? Was it too much today? You look tired. Are you sure you're okay?"

I assured her I was fine, even though I knew she wasn't convinced. She looked at me like I was a puzzle she couldn't quite solve, a fragile thing she had to handle with care. I wanted to tell her that I felt good, that I was proud of myself, that I didn't need to be watched over every second. But I knew she wouldn't understand. She saw the world differently when it came to me, as though I were made of porcelain, ready to shatter at the first sign of trouble.

As the weeks went by, I started getting into the rhythm of things at work. I got better at handling the busy nights when the lobby was full and the lines stretched all the way to the door. I learned to tune out the chaos to focus on each order, one at a time. I felt the confidence growing inside me, like a spark that was finally being fanned into a flame. I started to believe in myself and my ability to manage on my own.

One night, during a particularly busy shift, I was working the register by myself. The theater was packed; people were in a rush to get their snacks and drinks, and the orders were coming at me fast. My hands were moving almost automatically—popcorn, soda, candy, repeat. And then, out of the blue, the register jammed. The line was growing, people were getting impatient, and I could feel the pressure building in my chest.

Matt was busy helping another worker, so I was on my own. My heart started pounding; my hands shook as I tried to figure out what to do. I took a deep breath, forcing myself to stay calm, to remember everything Matt had taught me. After a few tries, I managed to fix the problem, and the register beeped back to life. I let out a sigh of relief, feeling a surge of pride. I'd done it—on my own.

When Matt came over later, I told him what had happened, expecting him to maybe say something reassuring. Instead, he just shrugged and said, "Good job, Jonathan. You handled it." It was a simple statement, almost offhand, but it meant everything to me. No big fuss, no words of concern. Just an acknowledgment that I'd handled it. And that was all I'd wanted.

As I kept working, those small victories piled up, each one adding a little more weight to my confidence. I learned to trust myself in a way I hadn't before. I knew I could make mistakes and learn from them without feeling like I was letting everyone down. It was like I was finally breathing on my own, free of the invisible hand that always seemed to be holding me back.

But the hard part was knowing my family didn't see me the same way. To them, my job was a risk, a challenge that might prove to be too much. My mom's words, her constant reminders to "be careful," were like soft echoes in the back of my mind, making me question myself even when I knew I was doing well. Every time she said, "I'm so proud of you, Jonathan," there was an undertone of "but don't push yourself too hard."

There was one night in particular that stuck with me. It was a Friday, and the theater was packed. My shift had been long, and I was tired but happy, the kind of happiness that comes from knowing you've put in a good day's work. My mom was waiting for me outside, like always, but this time, as soon as I climbed into the car, she could see the exhaustion on my face.

She reached over, brushing my hair back in that motherly way she has. "Jonathan," she said softly, her voice full of that familiar worry. "I think maybe you should cut back on your hours. You don't have to prove anything to anyone. We love you just the way you are."

Her words hit me harder than I expected. I felt a lump rise in my throat, a mix of frustration and sadness that I couldn't quite explain. "Mom," I said, my voice trembling, "I want to work. I like it. I don't want to stop just because it's hard sometimes. Doesn't everyone get tired?"

She looked at me, her expression softening, but I could still see the doubt, the worry. "Yes, honey," she said quietly, "but not everyone has... what you have. We just don't want you to get hurt."

There it was again—the reminder of my difference, the subtle way she reminded me that I wasn't like everyone else. I looked out the window, blinking back tears, and for the first time, I didn't answer her. I knew she meant well, that she loved me, but her love felt like a weight, holding me down when all I wanted was to fly.

As the months went on, I began to see my job not just as a place to work but as a symbol of everything I wanted—independence, confidence, the chance to prove to myself and the world that I could stand on my own two feet. I realized that this was more than a job for me; it was a piece of my freedom, a step out of the protective bubble my family had built around me. And though it scared me to think about stepping further, it also excited me. I wanted to find my own path, even if it meant sometimes walking alone.

In the quiet moments, when the theater was empty and I was cleaning up after a long shift, I'd think about my future, about the kind of life I wanted to live. I wanted more than their love and concern; I wanted respect. I wanted to be seen as capable, as someone who could handle the world on his own terms. I knew it wouldn't be easy and that there would be struggles and setbacks, but for the first time in my life, I felt like I was ready to take that leap.

Longing For A Breakthrough

I didn't want to just be Jonathan, the one they protected. I wanted to be Jonathan, the one who made his own choices, who stood strong even when things got hard. And maybe, just maybe, one day, they'd see me that way too.

Chapter 3: The Family Business and Finding Purpose

Working in the family business was never just a job to me. It was a piece of my identity, a way to prove to myself and everyone else that I could hold my own. I wasn't just another employee; I was a part of something bigger, something my father had built from the ground up. Growing up, I'd watch him walk into his office, his expression calm and focused, his presence filling the room. He was the kind of man who commanded respect without saying a word, and deep down, I wanted to be like that.

When I joined the family business, I felt like I was taking on a legacy, carrying a torch that had been passed down. It was more than a paycheck—it was a chance to show that I belonged, not just as a member of the family but as an equal. I wanted my siblings to look at me the way they'd looked at our father, with that same respect, that same quiet admiration. I wanted to prove that I could handle the responsibility and that I could make a real difference.

But as much as I loved the work, it didn't take long for the cracks to show. I was given tasks, yes—bookkeeping and managing small parts of the operations—but it was always under watchful eyes. My siblings, especially my youngest sister, would control how I do things constantly, sometimes even redoing my work without telling me. I'd catch them looking over my shoulder, their brows furrowed, their voices filled with a concern that felt like a weight pressing down on me. They thought they were helping, but every time they double-checked my work, it felt like a reminder that they didn't fully trust me.

Longing For A Breakthrough

I tried to brush it off, to focus on the parts of the job that gave me pride. There was something deeply satisfying about balancing the accounts, watching the numbers line up, and knowing that I was contributing to the family's success. I'd stay late sometimes; however, as time passed, I ran the numbers again and again until I decided bookkeeping wasn't for me. I did want to take a step back and say, "I did that." I wanted my family to see my dedication and notice the care I put into every task, no matter how small. But the recognition I craved never seemed to come.

One day, my younger sister, who was a partner in the business, pulled me aside after a meeting. She was smiling, but her eyes were serious, the way they always were when she had something important to say.

"Jonathan," she began, her voice soft but firm, "we've been thinking… maybe it would be best if you focused on fewer tasks. We don't want you to feel overwhelmed."

The words hit me like a punch to the gut. I wasn't overwhelmed. In fact, I was handling everything just fine. I'd been putting in extra hours, doing my best to prove that I could keep up, but instead of seeing my dedication, all they saw was my supposed fragility.

"I'm not overwhelmed," I replied, trying to keep my voice steady. "I can handle it. I've been doing the bookkeeping for many years now. I've got it under control."

She looked at me, her expression softening with what I could only describe as pity. "We know, Jonathan. But sometimes… sometimes it's good to take a step back. We're just looking out for you."

Jonathan Winchell

Those words— "looking out for you"—echoed in my mind long after she walked away. I knew they meant well, but their concern felt like a shackle, keeping me from reaching my full potential. They couldn't see that I wanted more, that I was ready for more. To them, I was still the brother who needed extra care, the one they had to keep an eye on, just in case.

As the months passed, I found myself growing frustrated, my sense of purpose slipping through my fingers. I'd catch glimpses of my youngest sister in the office, the way she interacted with me, the discussions filled with a level of mistrust and disrespect that I longed to be a part of. They'd talk about business strategy, discuss investments, and make decisions that affected the future of the company. And there I was, managing the numbers and doing my part, but always on the outskirts, never truly part of the inner circle.

One afternoon, after a long day, I sat alone in the office, my hands resting on the desk, feeling the weight of my frustration pressing down on me. I wanted to be part of something more, to be trusted with real responsibility, to feel like an equal. I was tired of being seen as the one they needed to protect. I wanted to show them that I was capable, that I could handle the same challenges they did, and that I was more than my disability.

A few weeks later, an opportunity presented itself. I saw my youngest sister was having issues with my bookkeeping and mainstreaming the accounts. Fortunately, the numbers were fine. I saw my chance to step up to show them what I could do. I spent hours poring over the various accounts, and it wasn't about tracking down discrepancies and double-checking every line item; it was all about interpreting the financial reports that my youngest sister never shared with me. It was challenging, but I felt alive and focused in a way I hadn't felt in years. By the time I finished, my eyes were tired, and my head was spinning, but I felt a deep sense of pride.

The next day, I presented my work to my siblings, hoping they'd see the effort and the care I'd put into it. But instead of the praise I was hoping for, they looked at each other, worry flashing across their faces. My youngest sister pulled me aside, her voice low and gentle, as if she were talking to a child.

"Jonathan," she said, "we appreciate your hard work, but you shouldn't push yourself so hard. It's just… we don't want you to get hurt."

The words stung, a reminder that no matter how hard I tried, they'd always see me as someone who needed to be shielded, as someone who couldn't fully handle the world on his own. My pride crumbled, replaced by a hollow ache. I'd given my best and poured my heart into the work, but it still wasn't enough. To them, my efforts were just a risk, something to be managed, rather than a contribution they could respect.

I went home that night feeling defeated. I stared at my reflection in the mirror, wondering if maybe they were right, if maybe I was reaching too high, asking for too much. But then, somewhere deep inside, a voice stirred, a voice that had been growing stronger with every setback, every small victory. It reminded me of all the things I'd already accomplished, of the strength I'd found in myself despite the doubts, the barriers, and the quiet limits they placed on me.

They couldn't see my strength, but I could. I knew what I was capable of, even if they didn't believe in it yet. I knew I could handle more, that I could push myself further. I wasn't fragile. I wasn't weak. I was just

Jonathan Winchell

Jonathan, a person with dreams and hopes, with the same fire that burned in everyone else. And maybe that fire would take me places they couldn't imagine, places they didn't think I could go. But I would keep pushing, keep believing, because I couldn't live my life in the shadow of their doubt.

I realized then that if I wanted to be seen for who I truly was, I'd have to find my own way, step out of the family's safety net, and carve my own path. I wasn't giving up on them, but I was learning that my journey, my purpose, was mine to define. And maybe, just maybe, if I kept believing, kept trying, they'd one day see the person I was becoming—the person I'd always been.

Chapter 4: Health, Wellness, and Self-Care

My health—it's something I think about constantly, whether I want to or not. I used to take it for granted when I was younger, back when I could move freely and run around without a second thought. Back when my body felt strong and dependable, it was something I didn't have to worry about. But that changed. Over time, my body began to set its own limits, ones I didn't see coming. And as each new restriction crept in, I felt a piece of my independence slip away.

I was diagnosed with type 2 diabetes in 2014. It wasn't something that came as a total shock—I'd always struggled a bit with my weight, and I knew I hadn't been making the best choices when it came to food. But the diagnosis still hit me hard. It felt like my body was betraying me, like it was giving up on me before I was ready. Diabetes is one of those things that seeps into every part of your life, whether you like it or not. Suddenly, everything I ate became something I had to think about, to monitor, to calculate.

At first, I tried to manage it on my own, telling myself I could handle it and that I didn't need anyone else's help. But diabetes is sneaky—it doesn't give you a choice. I'd get these dizzy spells, feel lightheaded, my blood sugar dipping or spiking depending on what I'd eaten, or worse, what I'd forgotten to eat. And my family, of course, noticed. They were always watching, waiting for a sign that I was pushing myself too hard. Their concern was palpable, always lingering just under the surface, like an unspoken weight pressing down on me.

Jonathan Winchell

One evening, not long after my diagnosis, I felt myself starting to crash. I'd been so focused on work that I forgot to eat lunch, and now my blood sugar was plummeting. My hands were shaking, my vision was blurred, and I felt like I was underwater, my mind heavy and slow. I stumbled to the kitchen, grabbing the first thing I could find—an apple. But by then, my mom was already there, her eyes wide with worry.

"Jonathan, are you okay?" she asked, her voice trembling.

I managed to nod, trying to hide the frustration bubbling up inside me. I wanted to tell her that I was fine and that I didn't need to be fussed over, but the words got stuck. I could see the fear in her eyes, and it hurt to know that I was the cause of it. In moments like these, I felt more like a burden than a son. It's a terrible feeling, knowing that the people you love most see you as fragile, as something to protect.

After that day, I became more vigilant about my blood sugar. I carried snacks with me, set alarms on my phone to remind myself to eat, and did everything I could to avoid another scare. I wanted to prove to my family—and to myself—that I could manage this on my own. But the thing about diabetes is that it doesn't care about your plans. There are good days and bad days, and sometimes, no matter how careful you are, things go wrong.

A few years after my diagnosis, my health took another turn. My legs started to feel weak, my balance was off, and walking long distances became a struggle. Eventually, I needed a walker, something I never imagined I'd have to use. The first time I held that cold metal frame in my hands, it felt like a defeat. It was like my body was telling me, "This is your life now. This is what you have to accept." But accepting it felt impossible.

Longing For A Breakthrough

I wasn't ready to give up the freedom of movement, the simple joy of walking without a second thought.

When I showed up at a family gathering with the walker for the first time, I saw the way they looked at me. It was a mixture of sadness and pity, a reminder that they saw me as someone whose world was shrinking, not expanding. My sister pulled me aside, her voice soft, her eyes full of sympathy.

"Jonathan, if you need anything, just let us know," she said. "We're here for you."

I nodded, forcing a smile, but inside, I felt a familiar pang of frustration. I didn't want their pity. I didn't want them to see me as someone who needed help, someone whose life was now defined by limitations. I wanted to be seen as strong, as capable, as someone who could still take on the world, even if my body was changing.

But the truth was, my body was changing, whether I wanted to admit it or not. As the months went by, I started to accept the walker as part of my life, even though it never felt natural. And then, things took another turn. I'd been having trouble with longer distances, feeling pain in my legs, my feet tingling with pins and needles, but I tried to ignore it. One night, as I was getting ready for bed, I felt a sharp pain shoot down my spine, and the next thing I knew, I was on the floor. My legs had given out beneath me, and I couldn't get back up.

I remember lying there, staring at the ceiling, my mind racing with a mixture of fear and anger. I didn't want to call for help. I didn't want my family to see me like this, to see me helpless on the floor. But eventually, I had no choice. My mother found me, her face pale, her hands shaking as she helped me back up. After that, it was clear: I needed a wheelchair. The walker wasn't enough anymore.

Adjusting to the wheelchair was even harder than I'd expected. It wasn't just the physical limitation; it was the way it changed how people saw me and how they treated me. Suddenly, I was "disabled" in a way that felt more visible, more concrete. People looked at me differently and spoke to me differently, as if I were someone to be pitied or protected. And my family… well, they were supportive, of course. But their concern became even more intense, their worry more palpable. They hovered over me, always ready to step in, always ready to take over if I faltered.

One evening, I overheard my siblings talking in the kitchen. They were discussing my future and the possibility of moving me into a more accessible home, one where I could get around more easily. They spoke in hushed tones, their voices full of concern, but I felt like a ghost, like I wasn't really there. They didn't ask me what I wanted and didn't think to include me in the conversation. It was as if my life had become something they had to manage, something they had to control, even if it meant pushing me to the sidelines.

Hearing them talk that way hurt more than I could say. I wanted to shout, to tell them that I was still here, still capable of making my own choices, of deciding what kind of life I wanted to live. But I stayed silent, feeling the weight of their expectations pressing down on me. They meant well, of course. They wanted to protect me, to make things easier. But their love felt like a trap, a cage that kept me from living fully.

Longing For A Breakthrough

As time went on, I started to adapt to the wheelchair, learning to navigate the world in a new way. But every time I ventured out, I was reminded of the obstacles, the lack of accessibility, and the way the world isn't built for people like me. Ramps were too steep, doors too narrow, and bathrooms inaccessible. Everywhere I went, there were reminders that I didn't quite fit, that the world saw me as someone who didn't belong.

However, despite the frustrations and the limitations, I refused to give up. I started seeing a physical therapist, working on exercises to strengthen my legs, hoping to regain some of the mobility I'd lost. It was hard, grueling work, and there were days when I wanted to give up when the pain and exhaustion felt like too much. But I kept going, driven by a quiet determination to reclaim some part of myself, to prove that I was still capable, still strong.

My family, of course, worried about the therapy. They thought I was pushing myself too hard and that I should just accept my limitations and focus on "quality of life." But for me, this was quality of life. It was the ability to hold onto some piece of my independence, to fight for my own future, even if it looked different than I'd imagined.

One day, after a particularly intense session, I came home feeling both exhausted and proud. My muscles were sore, my legs shaky, but I'd managed to take a few steps without the walker. It was a small victory, but it felt monumental to me. I wanted to share it with my family, to show them that I was still capable of progress, still capable of pushing my limits.

When I told them, though, I could see the worry in their eyes, the way they looked at each other, their faces full of concern.

Jonathan Winchell

"Jonathan, maybe you shouldn't push yourself so hard," my mom said gently, her voice filled with love but also with doubt.

I felt a familiar frustration rising up inside me, a mix of anger and sadness that they couldn't see what this meant to me. I wanted to shout, "I'm not fragile! I'm not someone who needs to be saved!" But instead, I just nodded, forcing a smile, and told them I'd be careful.

That night, as I lay in bed, my mind kept turning over the same thoughts. I thought about everything I'd lost and the things I was still holding onto, even if just by a thread. My family's worry and protectiveness were part of them, part of how they showed love, but it felt like a chain around my ankles. I knew they meant well, but they couldn't see how it kept me bound, unable to fully spread my wings and live on my own terms.

I knew my life would always have limits, but I wanted to decide where those limits lay. I wanted to prove, if only to myself, that I could keep pushing and moving forward. Yes, my body had changed, and yes, there were days when the weight of it all felt unbearable, but inside, I still felt that spark, that drive to hold onto who I was, to live with purpose and dignity.

As I lay there, staring up at the ceiling, I made a promise to myself. I would keep going, keep pushing through the doubts—my own and theirs. I would work hard, not because I needed to prove anything to them, but because I needed to prove it to myself. This was my life, my journey, and I wasn't going to let anyone else define what it meant to live fully, to be truly alive.

Maybe they would never understand; maybe they'd always see me as someone to protect. But that was okay. I was learning that my strength, my

Longing For A Breakthrough

sense of self, didn't have to depend on their approval. It was something I could carry on my own, quietly and proudly. And maybe, just maybe, that would be enough.

Jonathan Winchell

Chapter 5: Seeking Support and Connections Outside Family

For a long time, my world felt small, limited to the familiar faces of my family, my coworkers, and the doctors and therapists who monitored my health. My family was my constant, my home base, but they were also my safety net—always there, always watchful. It wasn't until I met Len in 1995 that I realized how much I needed something else, something outside of my family's cautious love. I needed someone who saw me for who I was, without the worry, without the protective walls. Before I had met Len, I knew Efi in 1993 and later I also did a volunteer project at the local movie theater.

Len was my first real mentor, and meeting him felt like stepping into a new chapter of my life. He worked as a volunteer director of the Bay Area Radio Hall of Fame, where I also volunteered, handling various events and programs. He was a tall, sturdy man with a calm presence and a wry sense of humor that could lighten up even the heaviest of days. Len treated me differently from the start—like an equal, like someone he respected. When he asked me to help with events, it wasn't because he thought I needed something to do or because he felt sorry for me. It was because he trusted me, genuinely trusted that I could handle the work.

The first time he assigned me to be a photographer for the California Historical Radio Society at one of the events, my nerves were buzzing. It was a lot of responsibility, and the crowd was big—mostly Bay Area Radio Hall of Famers and volunteers—all coming and going. I worried about making mistakes, about fumbling under the pressure. But Len just looked at me, his face calm, his voice steady.

Longing For A Breakthrough

"Jonathan, you've got this," he said, clapping a hand on my shoulder. "You're capable. Just stay focused and trust yourself."

Those words hit me like a wave, not because they were extraordinary but because of the trust he put in me. For the first time, someone outside of my family was giving me responsibility without reservation. He wasn't watching over my shoulder, waiting for me to make a mistake. He believed in me, and that belief filled me with a confidence I hadn't felt in a long time.

As the day went on, I found myself settling into the rhythm of the event. I greeted people, handed out tickets, directed others to the right spots, and answered questions. There were a few small hiccups, of course—a mix-up with a ticket order—but each time, I handled it. And when I looked up and saw Len watching me from across the room, his face was full of quiet pride, not pity or worry. In that moment, I felt seen, truly seen, for the person I was striving to be.

Over the months, Len became more than a mentor; he became a friend. He'd invite me out to get a diet coke after the volunteer work we both did, and we'd talk about everything—his family, my life, the world. He told me stories about his days regarding public relations in major league and minor hockey and taught me about statistics in other sports like the NFL, minor league soccer, and football, as well as about the places he'd gone to and the people he'd met. And each time he listened to my stories, he did so without judgment, without that look of concern I'd grown used to seeing in my family's eyes.

One evening, over a diet Coke, I decided to share something personal with him. I told him about my struggles with my family's protectiveness and how their love sometimes felt like a cage. Len listened, nodding quietly, his face thoughtful.

"You know, Jonathan," he said after a long pause, "sometimes the people who love us most don't realize they're holding us back. It's not their fault—they just don't see the strength we see in ourselves. But that doesn't mean you have to limit yourself to their expectations. You've got your own path to walk, and sometimes, that means stepping out on your own."

His words sank deep, giving voice to something I'd felt for years but had never been able to put into words. My family's love was a constant, a comfort, but it wasn't the only thing that defined me. There was a whole world out there, a life waiting for me if I had the courage to reach for it.

I knew Efi prior to Len through a volunteer project at the local movie theater.Efi was a bit of a character—sharp-witted, full of energy, with a mischievous smile that made you feel like you were in on a secret. He volunteered at the theater, organizing community events, and later, he brought his own movies over to a different location. Many years prior, he had also owned a computer store. When we met, he treated me like a friend, not as someone with a "condition" or a "special case." With Efi, I wasn't Jonathan, the one who needed looking after; I was just Jonathan, a person he enjoyed being around.

Efi had this way of seeing the world that was completely his own. He wasn't afraid to challenge people, to push them out of their comfort zones, and he never tiptoed around me or sugar-coated things. When he asked for my help with organizing a film event, he didn't hesitate to give me real tasks—managing the guest list, handling tickets, and setting up the venue.

Longing For A Breakthrough

He believed in me the same way Len did, and that belief made me feel stronger and more capable than I'd ever felt before.

One evening, as we were closing up after an event, Efi looked over at me, his eyes with that mischievous gleam.

"You know, Jonathan," he said, leaning against the counter, "you're more independent than you give yourself credit for. I see you doubting yourself sometimes, but you've got what it takes. Don't let anyone tell you otherwise."

His words stayed with me long after that night. In a way, they were simple and straightforward, but coming from him, that meant everything. He didn't see me as fragile or weak; he saw me as someone who could hold his own, who could contribute something real. With Efi, I felt like I could breathe and be myself without the constant weight of expectations and limitations.

As my friendship with Len and Efi deepened, I began to realize just how much I needed connections like these. They showed me a side of life I hadn't experienced before—a life where people saw me for my strengths, for my capabilities, not just for my challenges. With them, I felt free, unburdened by the weight of my family's cautious love. I felt like a person with dreams, with a voice, with a life that wasn't defined by my limitations.

But these friendships also brought a bittersweet truth into focus: the more I found acceptance and support outside my family, the more I realized how stifling their protectiveness had become. I knew they loved me, but their love was wrapped in worry, in a desire to protect me from the world. With Len and Efi, I didn't need protection. I was just me.

Jonathan Winchell

There was a day when Len and I were working on a project at the California Historical Radio Society, and he invited me to go to lunch at our friend's restaurant to talk about what he did in helping out with various responsibilities related to radio. My first thought was excitement, imagining what it is like talking about the radio, listening to the sounds of how it was in the 1940s and in the 1950s and even earlier, the freedom of the open trail where you don't want interference from the hills. But then, a familiar pang of doubt crept in. Would my family approve? Would they worry about me? I never let my limitations get to me because my volunteer work helped many people from the whole Bay Area in the radio industry. But my family did not understand that part.

When I mentioned it to my mom later, her face filled with concern. "Are you sure your wife wouldn't rather have you safe in her arms, Jonathan? Volunteering can take time away; however, you are doing what you like to do." When I mentioned to my mom that it is a safer activity where it is not strenuous, my mom responded, "Just be careful."

Her words felt like a cold splash of water, dousing the spark of excitement that had been growing in my chest. I wanted to tell her that I could handle it and that I wasn't afraid of a challenge. But the look in her eyes, that unspoken fear, held me back. I nodded quietly, pushing the dream of the hike to the back of my mind.

That weekend, I enjoyed my time alone with my wife at home, cooking together and watching television together, which felt very good. When I was at home with my wife, we showed pictures from our phones of the beautiful views and the joy of being in nature. I listened, smiling, nodding, but inside, I felt a hollow ache—a sense of longing for something I knew I couldn't fully have. I wanted the freedom to make my own choices, to take risks, to explore life on my own terms. And for the first time, I began to wonder if that freedom would always be just out of reach, hidden behind the walls my family had built around me.

However, despite the doubts and the limitations, my friendships with Len and Efi gave me strength. They reminded me that I was more than my family's concerns, more than their cautious love. I was a person with a heart full of dreams, with a will strong enough to face whatever challenges lay ahead. And maybe, just maybe, that would be enough to carry me forward.

One of the best parts of my friendship with Len was how he didn't shy away from challenging me. He treated me like someone who could handle life's ups and downs without needing a soft landing every time. Len had a way of pushing me out of my comfort zone, but always with a calm, steady hand. He never acted like he had all the answers, but his quiet confidence made me feel like I could find my own way as long as I trusted myself.

One of my favorite memories with Len was the day he invited me to join him at the California Historical Radio Society, where he was volunteering. It wasn't just any event; this was a massive gathering of radio collectors, enthusiasts, and families who came from all around. When he first told me about it, I felt a surge of excitement—and a hint of nerves. The idea of being part of such a big event thrilled me, but I couldn't help but wonder if I was truly up for the task.

The morning of the event, both Len and I showed up early; I tried to ignore the butterflies in my stomach. Len was busy setting up tables and directing volunteers, and when he saw me take on other responsibilities, he broke into a warm grin.

Jonathan Winchell

"Jonathan! Thank you for helping me out," he said, handing me a name tag. "We've got a lot of folks coming through today, so I need someone I can rely on to help with the entrance table. Think you're up for it?"

I felt a mix of pride and nerves swirl inside me. "I know so," I replied, sounding confident.

Len nodded. "Good. Just remember—you know this stuff better than anyone. If anyone's got questions, you'll have the answers. And if not, well, you'll figure it out." He gave my shoulder a reassuring squeeze before moving on to the next task.

As people started trickling in, I found myself settling into the role, greeting guests, directing them to different tables, and even striking up conversations about the various radio collections. Every now and then, I'd catch Len glancing over, giving me a thumbs-up or a quick nod of encouragement. He never hovered, never interfered—just kept his presence close enough that I knew he believed in me. And that made all the difference.

Halfway through the day, a young adult came up to the entrance table, his eyes wide with excitement. He struck up a conversation with me about sports, and we talked about a hockey card. He was maybe thirty-five to forty years old, with a shock of messy hair and a worn hockey cap pulled low over his eyes.

"Excuse me, sir," he said, looking up at me with all the seriousness an adult could muster. "Is there anyone here who can help me figure out if this card is valuable?"

Longing For A Breakthrough

I glanced down at the card—a classic from the '70s, worn at the edges but clearly loved. I smiled, feeling a warmth settle over me. "Well, let's take a look," I said, beckoning him over to the table. We spent the next few minutes examining the card, discussing its history, and talking about hockey. For those few moments, it didn't matter that I was at the front of a busy event or that I was "different" in the eyes of others. I was just Jonathan, sharing something I loved with someone else who cared just as much.

When the day finally wound down, Len came over, clapping a hand on my shoulder. "You did great today, Jonathan. I couldn't have asked for a better partner," he said, his voice warm with pride. And as we packed up, I felt a quiet joy settle in my chest. For once, I wasn't the one being taken care of. I was the one contributing and making a difference.

My friendship with Efi was different from the one I had with Len, but it was just as meaningful. Efi had this incredible ability to see right through people, strip away the pretenses, and find the truth beneath. With him, there was no sugar-coating, no careful tiptoeing. He was direct, honest, and sometimes even blunt, but I appreciated that about him. He never held back because of who I was and never treated me like someone who couldn't handle the truth.

One night, after a long day of volunteering at the movie theater, Efi and I found ourselves sitting on a bench outside, watching the lights of the town flicker in the distance. It was one of those clear, quiet nights, the kind where every sound seemed sharper, every feeling more intense.

"Jonathan," he began, his tone unusually serious, "have you ever thought about what you want from life? I mean, really thought about it? Not what your family wants, not what everyone else expects, but what you truly want?"

The question caught me off guard. I stared at him for a moment, his face half-hidden in the shadows, his eyes with curiosity. No one had ever asked me that before—not like this, anyway.

"I… I don't know," I admitted, my voice barely more than a whisper. "I guess I want what everyone else wants. Independence. Respect. A life that feels… like mine."

Efi nodded, a small smile tugging at the corners of his mouth. "Well, you've got more of that than you think. You're braver than most people I know, Jonathan. You just need to start believing it yourself."

His words echoed in my mind long after that night. With Efi, I didn't feel like someone who needed to be shielded. He saw me as capable, as someone who could handle the hard truths, who could take on life's challenges without needing a soft landing. And that was a gift I hadn't realized I was missing.

One day, he invited me to join him at a local charity event he was organizing. He needed someone to help with managing the event setup, organizing supplies, and coordinating volunteers. I hesitated at first, nervous about the responsibility, but his confidence in me bolstered my own.

When I arrived, the place was buzzing with activity. Efi handed me a checklist and pointed me toward the tables that needed arranging. "I'll be running around, but I know you've got this," he said, flashing me a quick grin before disappearing into the crowd.

Longing For A Breakthrough

I threw myself into the work, feeling a mix of excitement and nerves. By the time the event started, I'd helped set up tables, organize supplies, and even solved a last-minute crisis with the sound system. Efi checked in on me occasionally, but he didn't hover or second-guess. He trusted me, and that trust made me feel like I was truly capable.

At the end of the night, Efi found me, a look of satisfaction on his face. "See?" he said, folding his arms and nodding approvingly. "You're a natural. I knew you could handle it."

His words filled me with a warmth that lingered, a quiet reminder that I was more than just the person my family saw, more than the sum of my challenges. With Efi and Len, I was allowed to be myself and test my limits without fear of judgment. They didn't coddle me, didn't try to shield me from the world. They let me face it head-on, with all its ups and downs.

Over time, these friendships taught me that I didn't need to be limited by others' expectations. I began to see that my path, my journey, was mine to shape. The world was still full of obstacles, still full of reminders that I was "different," but with Len and Efi by my side, I felt stronger and more resilient. I could face the challenges, not because I was fearless, but because I was finally starting to believe in my own strength.

In those moments with them, I felt like I was truly living. For the first time, I began to understand that my worth wasn't something others could define—it was something I carried within me, something only I had the power to embrace.

Jonathan Winchell

Chapter 6: Exploring Passions and Hobbies

If there's one thing I've always known, it's that passions are what make life richer and fuller. For as long as I can remember, I've had this natural pull toward things that sparked a sense of wonder or excitement in me. They weren't just hobbies or interests; they were pieces of who I was, windows into a world that felt like mine and mine alone. And in a life often defined by what others thought I could or couldn't do, my hobbies became my sanctuary, a place where I could truly be myself.

One of my oldest passions is collecting sports memorabilia. I think it started when I was a kid, sitting on the couch with my dad, watching baseball and football games, and hearing him talk about the legends of the sport. He'd tell me about players from years before my time—not so much about the record-breaking games and the unforgettable plays, like my friend Len did in the previous chapters. There was something magical about those stories, something that made me feel connected to a legacy much bigger than myself.

When I got my first hockey card—a 1979-80 Topps card of Wayne Gretzky—I knew it was the beginning of something special. I remember holding that card in my hand, feeling the smoothness of the paper, and seeing the colors pop against the black background. It wasn't just a piece of cardboard; it was a piece of history, a reminder of a moment in time. From then on, I started collecting, saving up every bit of money I could to buy new cards, scouring garage sales, hunting down deals online, and going to card shows.

Longing For A Breakthrough

Over the years, my collection grew, expanding to include not only hockey cards but also signed baseballs, old jerseys, and even a few pieces of stadium memorabilia. Each item had a story, a piece of the past that I could hold in my hands. It was more than just collecting things; it was a way of holding onto memories, of preserving something that felt timeless. Whenever I felt overwhelmed or trapped by life's challenges, all I had to do was look at my collection, and a sense of calm would settle over me.

My love for sports also brought me closer to Len, who shared my passion for statistics and the stories behind the game. He was the one who introduced me to the world of sports card shows, where collectors from all walks of life came together to trade, buy, and talk about their favorite pieces. Going to those shows felt like stepping into a different world, a place where my disability didn't matter, where all that counted was my knowledge and love for the game. Len would introduce me to other collectors, and they'd treat me as an equal, listening to my insights and asking for my opinions. In those moments, I felt a surge of pride, a reminder that I had something unique to offer.

My other great love was film, especially the classic movies from Hollywood's golden age. There was something mesmerizing about the black-and-white films, the way the actors seemed larger than life, the way the stories unfolded with a kind of magic you don't see as often today. My love for movies eventually led me to volunteer at the local theater, where I met Matias, a film enthusiast who quickly became a friend. Matias knew everything there was to know about movies—directors, actors, cinematography, you name it. He'd light up whenever he talked about his favorite films, his eyes sparkling with enthusiasm, and I found myself soaking up his knowledge like a sponge.

Jonathan Winchell

One evening, Matias invited me to show me how he organized his classic film at the theater, a project he'd been passionate about for years. He spent hours putting together the lineup, choosing films that would appeal to audiences of all ages, and discussing every detail—from the sound quality to the size of the theater screen back in the 1950s and earlier. The night of the event, the theater was packed, and as I stood there, watching people settle into their seats, I felt a sense of pride and excitement that was hard to put into words. I was part of something bigger, a piece of the community, and for once, I didn't feel different or out of place. I felt like I belonged.

But perhaps my most unique passion—the one that's been with me through thick and thin—is my love for radio. When I was a teenager, my parents talked to me about how they listened to the radio. My dad remembered The Shadow on an old radio set that was heard back in the day. I am sure it didn't matter to him about the vintage models with the dials and knobs that took some real effort to tune. I'd just spoken to him about my interest in spending hours turning the dial, listening to the voices and music that floated through the static. There was something magical about it, the idea that I could connect with voices from miles away, that I could be part of a world beyond my own four walls.

Over time, I became fascinated by how radio worked. I learned about frequencies, antennas, and transmission waves, diving into the technical side of things with the same enthusiasm I had for sports and film. Eventually, I always dreamed about interning and started volunteering at a local radio station, doing whatever odd jobs they needed—cataloging records, organizing the studio, even getting on air occasionally to introduce a song or share a bit of trivia. The feeling of sitting in the studio, headphones on, microphone in front of me, was exhilarating. It was like stepping into another world, a place where my voice mattered, where I could connect with people I couldn't even see.

My family, of course, was supportive of my hobbies, but they didn't always understand the depth of my passion. To them, my collections, my movie nights, and my time at the radio station were just activities to keep me busy, things that gave me something to do. But to me, they were much more than that. They were my way of expressing myself, of showing the world who I was beyond the labels, beyond the limitations others tried to place on me.

One evening, after a long day at the theater, I came home and found my mom in the kitchen. She was making dinner, her face thoughtful as she stirred a pot on the stove. She looked up as I walked in, giving me a tired smile.

"You really love this film work, don't you?" she asked, her voice gentle.

I nodded, feeling a warmth spread through my chest. "Yeah, Mom. I do. It makes me feel... alive. Like I'm part of something."

She watched me for a moment, her eyes softening. "I know you're doing great things, Jonathan. I just... I worry sometimes. I don't want you to get disappointed if things get too hard."

Her words were meant kindly, but they carried a familiar weight, the same weight I'd felt so many times before. I knew she meant well, but I couldn't help but wish that, just once, she'd see my passions for what they were—a part of me, a testament to my independence, my strength.

But no matter what anyone thought, I knew the truth. My passions were my lifeline, my way of carving out a place in a world that often seemed to push me to the side. They were reminders of who I was, of the things I could achieve, the dreams I could pursue. And as long as I held onto them, I knew I'd be okay.

My collections, my movie nights, my time at the radio—they were more than just hobbies. They were pieces of my identity, reminders of a life I was building for myself, one step at a time. And with each day, each event, each moment of connection, I felt myself growing stronger, more certain of who I was and what I could become.

In a life filled with obstacles and challenges, my passions were the one thing I had full control over. They were my escape, my joy, my proof that I was more than just my limitations. And no matter what the future held, I knew they'd be with me, guiding me forward, one hobby, one passion, one dream at a time.

Hobbies are what make me feel alive, like I'm more than the limitations others see. For me, they're not just ways to pass the time; they're pathways into worlds where I feel strong, where I belong, and where I can be fully myself. Each one brings something different to my life, but they all give me the same feeling of freedom, a way to reach beyond the walls of caution my family built around me.

One Saturday morning, I woke up early, buzzing with excitement for the local sports memorabilia convention. I'd been saving for weeks to add a new piece to my collection, something special to remind me of a time or player I admired. The conventions weren't just about the memorabilia—

they were like gatherings of people who spoke the same language and shared my passion for every aspect of the game.

Len had arranged for both of us to drive in one car at the convention, and when we both walked in, Len had a coffee in hand while I had a hot chocolate in hand and stood among rows of tables covered in jerseys, balls, and autographed photos. He waved me over, his eyes lighting up when there were hockey cards from the 1950's and the 1960's.

"Jonathan!" he called out. "You're just in time. I was scoping out a booth with some rare '50s and '60s hockey cards I thought you'd like."

We headed over to the booth together, where bunches of collectors were displaying rows of pristine, vintage cards from different decades. My heart raced as I scanned the collection. There, among the treasures, was a Gordie Howe 1951 rookie card—one I'd been hoping to add to my collection for years. I could feel a thrill build inside me, the kind that reminded me why I loved this hobby so much. It wasn't just about owning a piece of sports history; it was about feeling connected to something bigger than myself.

Len must have noticed my excitement because he nudged my shoulder, grinning. "Go on, Jonathan," he encouraged me. "Ask about it."

Taking a deep breath, I approached various hockey collectors, feeling a rush of pride as I shared my knowledge of the player and the game. Hockey collectors listened, nodding, and then started sharing stories about the era, the players they'd met, and the games they'd seen live. We swapped stories, our voices blending in with the hum of the convention, and for once,

Jonathan Winchell

I didn't feel like the person people were concerned about. I was just another collector, another enthusiast.

I wish I bought the card; Len did say you will eventually get it by saving up. Len gave me a thumbs-up; his encouragement gave me a sense of pride. As we walked out, I felt a sense of accomplishment—not just because I'd not get that item into my collection, but because I'd done it on my own terms, with a confidence that was truly mine.

But if my love for sports brought excitement, my passion for film brought a different kind of wonder. There's something timeless about the old movies, the ones shot in black-and-white, where every frame seemed crafted with care, every line delivered with conviction. Through film, I could step into another world, even if just for a couple of hours, and feel like I was part of something extraordinary.

At the local theater, I began volunteering at special events, helping by greeting others for film days and nights, and I would like to eventually give introductions before screenings. Matias, my friend at the theater, had a knack for curating the perfect lineup—everything from 1941 to curating and presenting a series of classic films at the Orinda Theatre. I like movies from the golden era and how they were shown: with short subjects and vintage previews. I hope one day I can introduce one of my favorite films, It's a Wonderful Life, to the audience.

"Jonathan, you know this movie inside and out," Matias said with a grin. "Who better to set the stage than you?"

The thought of standing in front of a crowd was nerve-wracking, but the chance to share my love for the film outweighed my nerves. When the night arrived, I walked onto the stage, feeling the warmth of the lights and the quiet anticipation of the crowd. I took a deep breath and began to talk about why the movie meant so much to me, about its message of hope, community, and the power of one person to make a difference. As I spoke, I felt a calm settle over me, as though I belonged there, sharing something I loved with others who would understand.

After the screening, a few people approached me, complimenting the introduction, asking questions, and sharing their own memories of watching the movie. For those brief moments, I was more than Jonathan with Mosaic Down syndrome; I was Jonathan, the film lover, the guy who could talk about old movies and make people see why they were still relevant.

And then, there was my old radio. I'd loved it since I was a teenager—that vintage set with its dials. I only hoped there was no static. Radio felt like magic—a way to connect with voices from far away, a reminder that there was a world out there beyond my own. Over time, I'd learned about frequencies, transmissions, and radio waves. I wish I had interned at a small radio station, where I could help organize records, edit clips, and sometimes, if I was lucky, host a short segment on the air.

I hope one day I can do a live broadcast so I will know how to adjust the microphone, practice my voice over the air, and wait for the signal to start. I'd like to eventually plan my segment carefully—a tribute to some of the greatest radio broadcasters of all time, voices I'd grown up listening to. As I spoke into the microphone, I imagined the listeners out there, people I couldn't see but who were tuning in, hearing my voice, and feeling the same love for radio that I did. It was like reaching across miles of distance and making a connection, even if only for a few minutes.

Jonathan Winchell

My family was always supportive, of course, but there were times when I could tell they didn't fully understand what these passions meant to me. To them, they were just ways to keep me busy, distractions to fill my time. But to me, they were more than that. They were lifelines, proof that I could live fully, explore deeply, and connect with the world around me.

One evening, after coming home— as I always imagined—I found my dad sitting in the living room, flipping through a photo album. He looked up as I walked in, his eyes thoughtful.

"Jonathan, you've got a real talent for this," he said quietly. "Your mom and I have been talking, and we're proud of everything you're doing. But we just want to make sure you're not overdoing it."

I could feel the familiar frustration bubbling up inside, but I took a breath, reminding myself that they only wanted the best for me.

"Dad," I said softly, sitting down beside him, "these things... they're more than just hobbies. They're my passions. They give me purpose. They make me feel like I'm part of something."

He looked at me for a long moment, his face softening. "I get it, son. I really do. But just remember—we're here for you. If it ever feels too much, don't hesitate to let us help."

I nodded, appreciating his concern but also knowing that these were things I needed to do for myself on my own terms. My hobbies were my expression, my identity, and a way to reach beyond the limits that others placed on me. And no matter what the future held, I knew I'd hold onto them because they were my proof that I could live fully, that I could be more than the labels others tried to put on me.

Longing For A Breakthrough

Whether it was sports cards, classic films, or the crackling voice on the radio, these passions kept me going, pushing me to reach higher, dream bigger, and believe in my own strength. They were mine, and no one could take them from me.

Chapter 7: The Emotional Impact of Disability

There's a certain kind of strength that comes from knowing yourself, from seeing your life with clear eyes and understanding what you're up against. I didn't come to that understanding overnight, and sometimes, it feels like I'm still learning. But if there's one thing I've realized, it's that my life is more than just a series of limitations. Yes, I was born with Mosaic Down syndrome. Yes, there are things I struggle with that most people never think twice about. But that doesn't make me any less whole. It just means I'm fighting battles that aren't always visible to others.

For as long as I can remember, I've had this awareness that people see me differently. My family, my friends, and even strangers all look at me with a mixture of kindness and caution, as if they're always ready to step in and always ready to catch me if I fall. I appreciate their support, truly. But what they don't see is that I'm capable of catching myself. I know how to stumble, how to fall, and how to get back up, even when it hurts.

One of my biggest tests was when I started working at the family business. The work itself wasn't too difficult, and I enjoyed being part of something bigger, something my father had built with his own hands. But the real challenge was facing the doubt I felt coming from my family. They meant well, of course, but their concern felt like a weight pressing down on me, a reminder that they saw my role as something fragile, something that could break under pressure. I wanted so badly to prove them wrong, to show them that I could handle it, that I could contribute in a meaningful way.

Another challenge that's shaped me is my health. Diabetes, mobility issues, and the physical challenges that come with Mosaic Down syndrome—each of these is like a battle I face daily. I can't deny that it's hard, but I also know that every time I push through, every time I manage my health, I'm proving to myself that I am stronger than I look. There are days when my body feels like it's fighting against me, when my legs ache, and my energy dips, but I don't let that stop me. I refuse to let my health define me, to let it tell me what I can and can't do.

I remember one particular day, a few months after I started physical therapy. My therapist had been pushing me to work on exercises to strengthen my legs, exercises that were painful and exhausting. I could feel the strain in every muscle, the ache that told me I was pushing my limits. There was one exercise—as I was walking up and down a hill using my walker at a slow but steady pace—it felt like climbing a mountain. I wanted to stop, to give in to the pain, but I kept going, telling myself that I could handle it.

"Come on, Jonathan," my therapist encouraged, her voice steady but firm. "Just a few more minutes. You're stronger than you think."

I took a deep breath, focused on each step, and pushed through the pain. When the timer finally went off, I stepped off the treadmill, my legs shaking and my heart pounding, but I felt a surge of pride. I had done it. I had faced the pain, faced the limitations, and I hadn't given up. Moments like these remind me that strength isn't always about physical power—it's about perseverance, about refusing to let your challenges dictate your life.

I carry that strength with me, even on the days when doubt creeps in. It's not that I don't have moments of frustration or sadness; I do. There are times when I feel the weight of my disability more than others, times when I wish things were different. But those feelings don't define me. I let myself feel them, let myself acknowledge the hardship, and then I keep moving forward. I've learned that strength doesn't mean ignoring the difficulties; it means facing them with courage, knowing that I'll come out stronger on the other side.

One night, after a particularly tough day, I found myself sitting alone in my room, thinking about everything I'd been through—the small victories, the setbacks, the moments when I'd felt unseen or underestimated. I could feel a quiet frustration building up inside me, a mix of anger and determination. I didn't want to be seen as someone who needed constant help. I wanted people to see my resilience, my strength, and the battles I faced every day without complaint.

"Why does it have to be this way?" I whispered, letting the frustration out in the silence of the room. "Why can't they see that I'm strong enough to handle this?"

As I sat there, a realization washed over me. I didn't need anyone else to see my strength for it to be real. The only person who truly needed to believe in me was me. I took a deep breath, feeling a sense of peace settle over me, and I knew that I could keep going and keep facing whatever life had in store because I had that faith in myself.

People often talk about resilience, about the ability to bounce back, to keep moving forward no matter the odds. I don't think it's something you're born with; it's something you build, piece by piece, through every challenge, every victory, every scar. My life has taught me that resilience isn't just about surviving; it's about thriving, about finding joy and purpose even in the face of difficulty.

Longing For A Breakthrough

With each challenge I face, I feel myself growing stronger and more grounded in who I am. My disability is a part of my story, yes, but it's not the whole story. I am Jonathan, a person with dreams, passions, and a spirit that refuses to be broken. I know that my path may look different from others, but it's my path, one I walk with pride and determination.

I think of my friends—Len, Efi, Matias—who see me for who I am and believe in my strength, even when others don't. They remind me that I am not alone and that I am supported, respected, and seen. And in moments when my confidence wavers, when I feel the weight of the world pressing down on me, I think of the times they've trusted me, the times they've stood by my side, and I find the courage to keep going.

There's a quote I once came across that I hold onto: "Strength grows in the moments when you think you can't go on but keep going anyway." That's what my life has taught me—to keep going, to keep fighting—because I owe it to myself to live fully, to be the person I know I can be. My disability may be part of my journey, but it doesn't define the destination.

So I move forward, not with the certainty of an easy path, but with the certainty of my own strength. I am a warrior in my own right, facing each day with courage, knowing that every step I take is a step toward a life lived on my terms. And no matter what lies ahead, I know I have what it takes to meet it head-on, with resilience, with faith, and with a heart full of determination.

Jonathan Winchell

Chapter 8: Struggles with Mobility and Accessibility

One thing I've learned over the years is that real strength doesn't come from having an easy path. It comes from adapting, from finding my own way even when the road is bumpy, and even when there are obstacles you didn't expect. I've faced many such obstacles, especially as my mobility has changed over time. Some days are harder than others, but I've learned to keep going and to find ways to live fully, even if that means doing things a little differently.

My mobility challenges have been a journey in themselves. In my younger years, I could move around with ease, run, play, and explore. But as I got older, things began to shift. I started feeling weaker, noticing the strain on my muscles and joints. It was subtle at first; there was just a little ache here and a bit of fatigue there. But eventually, it grew into something I couldn't ignore.

The day I started using a walker was a day I won't forget. It felt like a turning point, a reminder that my body was changing in ways I couldn't control. I wasn't thrilled about it, but I didn't let it get me down. I told myself that this was just another tool, another way to help me keep moving and keep exploring. And even though it took time to adjust, I made it work. I adapted, figuring out ways to stay active, even if I had to slow down a bit.

But just as I was settling into a new rhythm, I faced yet another shift—the need for a wheelchair. This change hit harder than the walker did. With the walker, I could still stand tall and feel like I was walking my own path. But the wheelchair was different. It felt like my independence was slipping away, like my body was telling me to sit back and slow down, even though my spirit wanted to keep pushing forward.

I'll admit there were moments of frustration, even anger. I'd think about all the places I wanted to go, all the things I wanted to do, and the limitations I now faced. Simple events and outings become complex. Something as basic as going to a grocery store wasn't as easy as it used to be—suddenly, I had to think about ramps, doorways, table heights. There were places I wanted to visit that weren't accessible, stairs that stood in my way, and narrow hallways that made me feel boxed in. I wanted to shout, "Why isn't the world built for people like me?"

But I realized that frustration wouldn't get me anywhere. I had two choices: I could let these obstacles hold me back, or I could find ways to work around them. And if there's one thing I've learned, it's that I don't like letting anything hold me back. So, I began to approach each challenge with a different mindset, seeing it as an opportunity to find new ways to live fully. I started researching accessible places and made lists of cafes, parks, and museums where I knew I could move freely. I even joined a few online groups where people shared tips and resources for accessible travel, connecting with others who understood the same challenges I was facing.

I also started advocating for myself more, speaking up when places didn't accommodate my needs. If I noticed a building without a ramp or a bathroom that wasn't accessible, I'd talk to the manager, calmly explaining the importance of these changes. It wasn't always easy, and I could tell that some people didn't quite get it, but I felt a sense of purpose each time I made my voice heard. I wasn't just standing up for myself—I was standing up for others like me who deserved the same freedom and ease of movement.

Jonathan Winchell

One day, Len invited me to a community event as we were volunteers of the Pleasant Hill Chamber of Commerce at the park, a big festival with music, food trucks, and games. I was excited, but I knew that a busy outdoor event might be a challenge. I did my research, called the event organizers, and asked about accessibility. I wish I could say, to my relief, they'd made arrangements for wheelchair access. Unfortunately, it wasn't happening, so I decided my limitations got the best of me because I didn't have an electric wheelchair to get around at that time.

I took my walker through the park, taking in the sights, the sounds, the smells of different foods cooking. People were everywhere, laughing, chatting, walking, and enjoying the sites. And in the middle of it all, I felt free. I knew that taking my walker was going to be a challenge. I still went around with my limited mobility, and I still enjoyed the outdoors, ate, and listened to music. I was out less than an hour, and I wasn't navigating my barriers that well—I was just Jonathan, enjoying the day.

After the festival, I felt a renewed sense of determination. I knew that life would continue to have challenges, but I wasn't going to let them stop me. I made a promise to myself: I would keep exploring, keep pushing the boundaries, and keep finding ways to live fully, regardless of what obstacles lay ahead.

Another part of adapting to these changes has been physical therapy. It's not easy work, but it's become an essential part of my routine. My therapist, Bri, has been with me since the beginning, and she's taught me more than just exercises. She's taught me about resilience and the importance of moving forward, even when things get tough. Each session is a reminder that my body is capable of more than I sometimes give it credit for. It may take extra effort, but I know that every stretch, every movement, is a step toward strength.

"Remember, Jonathan," she said one day during a particularly tough session, "your strength isn't just in your muscles. It's in your willpower. As long as you believe in yourself, you'll keep finding ways to move forward."

Her words have stayed with me, a reminder that strength isn't just physical—it's also mental. Every day, I remind myself that I have the power to adapt and find ways around any challenge that comes my way. My wheelchair may help me physically, but my spirit is what keeps me moving forward.

One evening, as I was reflecting on all the changes I'd been through, a thought struck me. I realized that I'd been focusing so much on what I couldn't do that I hadn't fully embraced what I could do. There were still adventures to be had, still new places to see, still moments of joy waiting for me. And I wasn't going to let anything get in the way of those moments.

So, I started making a list—a "bucket list" of sorts. I wrote down places I wanted to visit, activities I wanted to try, things I'd always dreamed of doing. I included simple things, like visiting a new restaurant, as well as bigger dreams, like going on a road trip with a friend. With each item I added, I felt a renewed sense of purpose, a reminder that my life was still full of possibilities.

As I looked at my list, I felt a wave of gratitude. I was grateful for my friends, at times with my family, for the strength that had carried me this far. I knew that I had a long road ahead, but I also knew that I was ready for it. I would keep adapting and finding new ways to live fully because that's

Jonathan Winchell

who I am. I am someone who refuses to be held back, someone who believes that life is worth living to the fullest, no matter the obstacles.

And with each day, each new experience, I feel that spirit growing stronger. My wheelchair may have changed how I move, but it hasn't changed where I'm going. I'm still on my path, still following my dreams, and nothing—no obstacle, no challenge—will stop me from living the life I've worked so hard to create.

Chapter 9: Forgiveness, Acceptance, and Moving Forward

As I look back on my life, I can see how far I've come. I see the battles I've fought, the doubts I've faced, and the victories I've achieved—some small, some bigger than I ever thought possible. It's funny how time has a way of showing you things you couldn't see before. For years, I thought my life was all about overcoming obstacles, about proving that I was more than what people saw on the surface. But now I understand that my life is about more than just challenges and victories. It's about growth, acceptance, and finding peace within myself.

For a long time, I felt like I was living in a glass box, surrounded by the world but not fully a part of it. People looked at me with kindness, yes, but there was always this sense of separation, as if I were someone to protect, to watch over carefully. They didn't see the strength I had inside; they didn't know the depth of my determination. To them, I was Jonathan, the one who needed help, who needed extra care. And in their own way, I know they meant well. But what they didn't understand is that I'm not made of glass. I may be different, but that doesn't mean I'm weak.

As I've grown, I've come to see my life as a tapestry woven from all the experiences, lessons, and people who have been a part of it. Every challenge, every setback, every small victory—they're all threads in the story I'm writing. And I've learned to take pride in that story, to embrace it as uniquely mine. I may not have followed a traditional path, but that doesn't make my life any less valuable or meaningful. In fact, I think it makes it more so because I've had to fight for every step, every piece of independence, every moment of self-discovery.

Jonathan Winchell

One of the biggest lessons I've learned is that acceptance isn't about giving up; it's about finding peace within yourself. For years, I thought acceptance meant surrender, that it meant settling for a life that others thought was good enough for me. But now I see that true acceptance is about recognizing your worth, about understanding that you are enough, just as you are. I don't have to prove my value to anyone; my life has value simply because it's mine.

This doesn't mean I don't still have dreams, ambitions, and goals. I do. In fact, I think I have more now than I ever did. But I've learned that my dreams don't have to be defined by anyone else's expectations. They're mine to shape, chase, and fulfill in my own way. And that realization has given me a sense of freedom, a sense of purpose that no obstacle can take away.

I used to feel a lot of anger toward the world, toward the people who saw me as fragile and who doubted my abilities. But over time, that anger has softened. I've come to understand that most people don't act out of malice—they act out of misunderstanding. They don't see the whole picture, and that's not entirely their fault. So, I've chosen to forgive, to let go of the bitterness that used to weigh me down. My life is too precious to waste on resentment. Instead, I choose to focus on what I can control, on the person I want to become.

There's a peace that comes with forgiveness, a lightness that I never thought I'd find. It's like a weight lifting from my shoulders, a reminder that I am not defined by the perceptions of others. I am defined by my choices, my values, my dreams. And as I move forward, I want to carry that peace with me, to let it guide me through whatever lies ahead.

Longing For A Breakthrough

One of the things I hope to share with the world is that being different isn't something to fear or pity—it's something to celebrate. My differences have taught me resilience, compassion, and courage. They've made me who I am, and I wouldn't trade them for anything. Yes, my life may look different from most, but it's a life filled with purpose, with strength, with love. And I wouldn't have it any other way.

In the coming months, I plan to continue working on my goals. I'm still saving up for my travels, exploring options for independent living, and finding ways to contribute to the community. Each of these steps brings me closer to the life I envision, a life where I am free to be myself, to live fully, and to experience the world on my terms. I know there will be challenges along the way—there always are. But I also know that I am ready to face them and that I have the strength to overcome them.

As I walk this path, I want to leave something behind, something that shows others that life is worth fighting for and that every person has value, no matter what challenges they face. My blog has become a place where I can share this message and connect with others who might be feeling the same struggles and doubts. I want my story to be a light, a reminder that strength doesn't come from having it easy—it comes from facing hard things with courage, from finding hope even when it seems out of reach.

My hope is that, by sharing my story, I can help change the way people see disability. I want them to understand that disability isn't a barrier to a meaningful life—it's just one part of a person's journey. We all have our own paths, our own battles, our own dreams. And we all deserve the chance to live those dreams, to make our own choices, to build our own lives.

Jonathan Winchell

So, as I close this chapter, I do so with a heart full of gratitude. I am grateful for the people who have believed in me, for the friends who have stood by my side, and for the lessons I've learned along the way. But most of all, I am grateful for the strength I've found within myself, the strength to keep going and to keep reaching for the life I want. I am not made of glass. I am not someone who needs to be protected from the world. I am someone who is ready to embrace it, to live fully, and to show others that life, no matter how different, is worth every moment.

As I look to the future, I see a world of possibility. I see new adventures, new friendships, and new chances to make a difference. And I am ready for it all. I may be different, but I am strong, capable, and full of hope. I am Jonathan—unique, resilient, and unbreakable. And as I move forward, I do so with the certainty that my life, with all its ups and downs, is a life worth living, a life I am proud to call my own.

Chapter 10: Interaction with my siblings

As time passed by working in the family business, I learned that my dad commanded respect. I felt after my dad passed away in October of 2007, after my 42nd birthday, it was like carrying a torch that had passed down. At times, it felt good doing things on my own and, at times, interacting with my siblings under watchful eyes, but I didn't like how I felt. It was very hard for me. I wanted my siblings to look at me the way they'd looked at our father. I wanted to prove that I could handle the responsibility and that I could make a real difference. It was then under watchful eyes that my siblings, especially my youngest sister, would control how I do things constantly without communicating and telling me. I didn't know at that time it may have caused her to have controlling characteristics, but I just didn't think much of it because I was so focused on the work at hand. It took a while till I realized I needed to find my own job without the family, and it turned out well. It was after a while that I found a job that I liked, working at a theatre in Concord. I worked there for two years; unfortunately, I didn't get support from my family because they wanted me to sacrifice my job to go on a family vacation. I was so pissed and expressed I hadn't worked that long, and they chose to have me make a decision between vacationing with the family or finding a job on my own that I was excited about. So, I decided to go on vacation despite my excitement about finding my own job on my own.

It was in 2016 when I found out eight years later, in 2024, that my family had a meeting without me regarding the family business with the accountants and lawyers. It was devastating, and that was the biggest elephant in the room at that time. In part, it was about my family not communicating with me, and in the meeting, it had to do with my sons where my sisters went along with what my mom did in making my sons' lives comfortable without telling me, and that shows my life is still being under control. As I look at my life from 2016 to now, there has been no structure, meaning there wasn't prioritizing in establishing a routine such as managing responsibilities, especially in dealing with family and siblings, which prevents me from feeling overwhelmed, including reducing my stress and improving my focus. I always felt that by being born with a disability, I showed how unpredictable I am by feeling a lack of security.

I had another problem: my brother and my mom relied on my sister to control my finances, especially limiting my credit card and how much they would pay when the payment was due. So when I communicated with my sisters about my medication being low and how my medication doesn't come on time, my brother and my mother went along with what my sisters do for me, and it stressed me out because they found it embarrassing for me to be vulnerable. I asked my sisters to help me out; unfortunately, no matter how hard I tried, my fears and anxiety issues increased. It was also due to my type 2 diabetes in addition to my health issues and concerns.

Even today, I try to eat healthy, and at other times, I go out because there are emotional triggers that set me off. I have to avoid my interactions with my family to the point where I have to limit how much time I want to spend with them. My life is too precious to waste on controlling issues with my mom and my siblings. Being the oldest of four children, there are more expectations because I am excessively expressive, and the more I do that to improve my social skills, the more my family interactions distance themselves from me. I like feedback and getting validation by speaking to my mom and my siblings about my first book. It wasn't an easy discussion because after I published it in 2022, they never read the book. I know after a while, my family has predisposed conceptions, perceptions, or both on what they think they know about me. I will say that under those circumstances, it is due to their conditional love and not unconditional love, which is hard for me to deal with and embrace, to say the least. In speaking about interacting with my mom and siblings, I see that they have controlling characteristics that lead to no boundaries and rules. My family always has something to say about how I lead my life, specifically how I need to have rules and expectations for my behavior and responsibilities, so I guess being born with a disability and being the oldest, they expected me to act a certain way. My mom would say, "I expect you to assume responsibility." I didn't want to say the idiom of assuming to my mom; in either case, I didn't like feeling foolish or embarrassed around my family. This is why I have always wanted to reduce my interactions with my family. I am very independent and versatile, whereas when I reach out to my family where, they keep things to themselves, such as setting their own boundaries and limiting me to what I should say around them, as they are very selective about what they want to hear. When I do get together for family occasions—it's been a while since I last did—they would rather see me than hear from me. It's basically just for appearances, and that's sad. It's hard at times to make time for myself and maintain my mental, physical, and emotional well-being around them.

I do have hobbies, but at the same time, it is hard to prioritize the other activities that will help me recharge and relax (like exercise and meditation due to my limited liability), and that's not by walking far due to me using my walker to get around. I don't like the increased stress and anxiety, as well as overwhelming feelings, lack of concentration, and focus, especially paying more attention to the source of my problems. My home life has not been created by consistent routines and rules.

Jonathan Winchell

To me, rules teach me as an adult like myself what behaviors are okay and not okay. As I write all of my thoughts down, I always ask myself what is okay and what is not. I want to know what to expect throughout the day. I share my problems from the past and present with my family. Unfortunately, since we all grew up together, that dynamic has evolved, and not for the better. What I have done to take care of myself is I always seek external support from friends and from therapy, especially after my dad passed away. I am becoming more self-aware that my life with my mom and siblings has been more complicated. For example, there have been more controlling issues by my mom and siblings where they need to control everything about me, and it can be all-consuming. I do have a more complicated issue that was recently brought up when talking to my boys, which I never thought to bring up because I grew up not to bring up my problems because my parents never talked about problems, and that includes behavior issues. If that's not a lack of structure, I don't know what it is. I always thought sharing is caring. I even share and talk about what's on my mind because it is very important for me to express myself. I like sharing despite my sons telling me they don't want to hear the dynamics of my family. I have never felt my behavior around my family is a healthy way to cope with difficult situations because I have always experienced a parent and my siblings micromanaging me.

As I write my thoughts down frequently as a form of expression, I am more aware that I handle difficult situations in a healthy way. I have always wondered why my family is more distant, knowing it is getting harder for me to trust my family when it takes a long time to interact with them. I feel my life is more rigid, and at times, when I discuss how I feel with my mom and my siblings, they are embarrassed to be vulnerable around me because I have a tough exterior on the outside. I have always shared and discussed how I felt, not because I am the oldest of four children but because I just find it invigorating that I can bring out the best in others because I have experience in being very sensitive on the inside and tough on the outside.

I experienced throughout my teenage and adult life that I was compared by my peers at a time in my life when I finished Junior High School in 1979 as a teenager. I was so frustrated and disappointed with my life because I knew I was different. I isolated myself because I had so many preconceived notions from a lack of motor skills, my speech and language, my cognitive and performance, and my activities of daily living. I have a skill set that is being controlled as I get older, and I don't fit in my surroundings, and that's my opinion. I didn't feel I fitted in because of my curriculum and my emotions in a healthy way were not controlled.

I never thought my mom ever micromanaged me, and with that said, I am more aware that my mom and my siblings just do not trust the decisions that I make for myself, and that hurts my feelings. I have always interacted with my family, and from 2016 to now, I can't allow myself to be involved in any family decisions because they take sides and show partiality. I don't like the feeling they are all against me just because they disagree with me. I have done so many good things on my own and accomplishments. I know my siblings don't compliment me on how I show my independence. I feel that when I am around my family, they only want to see me with rose-colored glasses and the limitations they put on me. I feel that the relationship between them and me is becoming thin. How does a Mosaic Down syndrome sibling like myself handle those challenges? I am a self-mover and have been very accomplished. As I read stories about Down syndrome, knowing that I have Mosaic Down syndrome, I didn't find any stories about parents or even adult children on how to handle Mosaic Down syndrome.

Jonathan Winchell

Being born with Mosaic Down syndrome and not having structure in my family upbringing, I don't like it when my family members tell me what I can and can't do. As I get older, I like to project a positive image. I hear from outside of my family that I am funny, witty, and very vocal, and the only thing that limits my life is my family questioning my beliefs.

So when my siblings put me in a position of what they think or know about me, they are projecting their own beliefs and imposing their own insecurities on me. I remember a time when I would call my siblings and see how they were doing and what they were up to, and this was prior to when they were married to their spouses. I know that has something to do with my interactions with my siblings; unfortunately, that's beyond my control. I also don't like it when my sisters need something from my wife, especially last-minute plans that they were doing for themselves and their spouses. I know they are going around me and talking to my wife to get what they want, like taking care of their house while they are gone. I get upset when they don't tell me what's going on, and I know I have to acquiesce on how I feel, which I never had to do before. I have physical limitations that I can or can't do; unfortunately, that doesn't mean my siblings should take advantage of me on what I can or can't do for me to get around, and they don't even ask me for help because they think I am helpless. In fact, being the oldest of four children, I need help from my siblings due to my own physical limitations in communicating. I still have problems from this morning, Saturday, March 15th, 2024. I needed help going to the doctor, but a few hours before the appointment, my mom called me and said you should do it yourself. I told her I couldn't walk like I used to.

Longing For A Breakthrough

Despite my physical limitations and what my family might do, it doesn't help that my family dynamics are getting more complicated. It is not just by telling me what I can and can't do; there are significant changes in my family structure, whether it is my relationships with my family or my individual roles with my siblings and especially their spouses when I am not informed due to what's in my own best interest and that's when I have no control. In my opinion, this can lead to new challenges and complexities in family interactions. I will say my two boys are very close with their cousins, so at least my next generation has a good and healthy relationship, of which I am very proud. My pattern is unhealthy due to me feeling isolated and rigid, which can negatively impact my family dynamics. I have accomplished a lot in my thirty years of working at my family business, and what I accomplished for my own well-being. I do acquiesce from time to time about what my role is now with my family. I always had conflicts at work in dealing with my youngest sister, as I acquiesced. I also know that my family shows bias and not so much questioning me but controlling me. Nowadays, it is more about controlling what I say and how I do things on my own so my family can limit their interactions with me just to avoid confrontation, and that is their way of being more distant from me.

It is clear to me I have focused more on being more sensitive on the inside. I don't like the feeling that my family is biased because that leads to jealousy. I don't want to show my lack of responsibility to my family or to others. I used to feel frustrated and isolated, and at times, that led to my disappointment but now I just shrug it off because I am around more people where I am providing a public service, which I need to do more of.

As time passes by, my emotions don't get the best of me because I feel more in control where I am distancing by feeling controlled and manipulated. I don't like how that feels. It is unfortunate that I feel passive in my writing, which makes me the victim of how I was treated, but that wouldn't be the whole story. I want my family to understand how I am still learning and want to fit in and have acceptance. I am still growing to be the best person I can be. I have also learned from my friends who are entrepreneurs that they accept me when I do things on my own and that it never came easy for me to do things on my own. I know that if I set my own boundaries and share them, it will be very empowering. When I revealed years of built-up grievances to my family, I was willing to provide more information to them as needed.

When I decided to spend time on my own, my family wanted me to be available, and I did exactly what I wanted, which was to show my independence and limit my interactions when things didn't go my way. I have got more control because I felt I was not caring for my emotions.

I know there is no secret sauce in handling family because you can't pick your family; however, I can take the high road and try to understand that I may feel ashamed, demeaned, and belittled just because of the circumstances. I just need to recognize that I must somehow hold onto my dignity. I just realized I can't choose my family, no matter whether I acknowledge them or not, because it will make me look silly. I want to show people around me that I have a positive attitude and that I will see how I feel towards them. I just have to show positive boundaries around my family as I get older. I acknowledge that my family relationship is complex and challenging as I may not get along with everyone in my family; however, I do have friends who share and understand me. I do interact with my family about my positive outlook. I have collaborated and acquiesced with my stories about my family in a good light. When I finished my first book,

Longing For A Breakthrough

Being Different Than My Family Living With Mosaic Down Syndrome Chromosome #21, in 2022, I felt being different was a good thing.

It provides me with more peace and more information about myself, where I love learning and being a highly functional adult. I also know by accepting that my family is too closely involved in my life, I feel they are very particular about what they want to hear from me, and it will eventually lead to no more emotional connection that I once had and once that happens my time with them won't be the same anymore. I feel that the emotional bond is gone, and I would feel uncomfortable and sad.

I do acquiesce to being around my family, which is very unsettling to me. I feel that no matter what I say to my family, the things that bother me the most are that I don't belong and that I am different. I also feel in the present situation in dealing with my family, they put me down, especially being compared to my sisters, and I feel being the oldest of four, I am always intellectually challenged because my family looks at me and communicates in a way that I can't take care of myself. In reality, here is another example of having a family that is controlling in my daily life, thinking I can't take care of myself when, in reality, they are all overprotective of their own emotional triggers. I even remember an experience way before my dad passed away on how my parents were so overprotective of my disability while we were all walking at the Lafayette Reservoir, and we saw my speech therapist.

I realized so many years after my dad passed away that dealing with people from the outside or even me questioning my interactions with my family has always been a struggle, to say the least. I guess I know that my family has been overprotective of me while, at the same time, they look down on other professions because they feel they are the only ones who can take care of me. I also have known after my dad passed away, things weren't the same. My mom showed more dependency and relied on my sisters, and at this time, my brother had lived his own life separately, living in a different state and only communicating when needed. Even now, he lives in the Bay Area, while I am living in the East Bay of Northern California. I have felt my family has unresolved conflicts with long-standing disagreements and unresolved issues regarding how to help me be highly functional with a disability where, in reality, being different is good, and that shows independence, which is a good quality.

I wish my family would understand me better as a mentally disabled kid, but my childhood is over. I wish there would be a general coming-of-age plotline or theme. I just need more people to talk to about my disabilities, and that includes me using a wheelchair where I can talk about myself. I have also got an issue with my Mosaic Down syndrome that is swept under the rug, and that can cause an illness and so many more. I want to learn more about it.

I just don't know who to reach out to. The challenge I have now is not to exacerbate my mental health issues like anxiety and depression. I even recognize my emotional triggers related to my mental health. It is a very painful and complex experience that I have, and my family still doesn't want to reconcile by engaging with me in honest, open communication. To me, it could be more serious as my family constantly criticizes my choices or refuses to follow the boundaries that I set. I have felt lately that these frustrating behaviors that I have for a prolonged period of time can lead to creating an unhealthy, loving family. I have always felt for a long time that I was always close to my family, which means interacting with them about family business decisions, but now it's all about focusing on my own well-being because my own sons rely on my sisters regarding my well-being. I am an adult and a parent to my sons, and I feel my sons seek support from my sisters and rely on them too much. This type of style is about controlling my behavior and not being supportive of my well-being without communicating with me. At least, that is their choice, which they abundantly tell me. So whether it's about business or personal, it just occurred to me as a teenager, and even as an adult, my family doesn't include me in decisions. It will eventually come down to having me focus on my own well-being as I acquiesce.

Jonathan Winchell

Chapter 11: Empowering My Independence

My journey is about embracing my life and reaching my fullest potential by taking risks outside of my comfort zone. I always enjoy challenges, especially keeping my mind active in handling various tasks without being demanded or reminded by anybody. That is where my normal cells took over my abnormal cells in being born with Mosaic Down syndrome. I enjoy taking responsibility for my actions because it assures me what needs to be done and not expecting someone else to do it for me. I also defer to my family's judgement, especially being semi-retired when it has to do with the day-to-day business operations and decisions, where I acknowledge and appreciate how they have helped me along the way.

I always found ways to create family cohesiveness by interacting with them on a personal level. I do acknowledge my family's decisions and opinions since we all had to work together after our father passed away in 2007. I always kept in touch with my family about the family business before my dad passed away, and being the oldest of four children, it was very hard at times because I was lonely and depressed. I felt I was in hibernation mode after my dad died. That is when I ate and ate excessively to the degree I became a type 2 diabetic. My family only looked at my disability as being developmentally delayed and due to me being a type 2 diabetic. I had to defer to my family's judgement in taking care of me so I could stay active when my quality of life wasn't the same. I also had challenges in staying fit because living my life wasn't easy. As time passed fast, I faced other challenges. What did that look like? I always wanted to be an athlete, knowing my education wasn't as good as it should be. I wanted to excel so badly in tennis, but I just never knew to what extent. I grew up taking private lessons because my parents didn't express any expectations and didn't share what demands were there in taking the next steps in furthering my athleticism. They just expressed to me that I wasn't good enough; they couldn't see the potential I had and visualize what the future could hold for me. My parents only saw the present in me and how difficult it was for me to be born with a disability. I am very proud that, in retrospect, I almost went to JV tennis in high school while I was in middle school, knowing that my parents were overprotective of me. I asked my parents if they wanted to play tennis with me. They just looked at me as their son instead of actively participating with me or showing any interest because, to them, it was more about me getting out as I wasn't social. What they did for me was give me private instructions from professional tennis instructors at the tennis court where I was growing up.

Yes, I was physically active and mentally prepared; I just wasn't sure what expectations my family had from me because they never demanded any. They just always worried, looking over their shoulder because I was born with a mental disability and not a physical disability. I grew up knowing that my family had misconceptions about my disability because it was overshadowed by Down syndrome. When my dad passed away, my siblings treated me the same way, with many misconceptions, and were not patient with me. My parents, when my dad was alive, didn't even know how to handle my type of disability, which is very different and unique, and they didn't even communicate with me. I was always questioning myself about being born with Mosaic Down syndrome and my abilities as a teenager in the late 70s because I always thought my abilities were hidden and not fully functional. I realized a lot later in life my parents only looked at my abnormal cells and not my normal cells because it wasn't fully developed, and at times, my family didn't give me enough attention because those challenges I had were insurmountable to say the least. I wish my challenges were sustainable. It is fortunate I was very highly functional, and I didn't even know at that time why I got so excited thinking it was my disability and I was just overly sensitive and overreacted. It became more transparent as I got older that my normal cells took over my abnormal cells.

I always wished my parents and siblings understood what I was going through. Unfortunately, the old saying is true: don't judge someone until you've walked a mile in his shoes. My family never had a disability, and I was the only one, being the oldest of four siblings, who had it. I have always felt that back then and in the present, my independence is full of conditions because I have always had challenges where I never had full power over my independence, so I can eventually have full autonomy in what goes on with me.

Without sounding glib or showing my knowledge, I have always been logical, reasonable, and showing my emotions because I have learned to embrace my feelings where they had nothing to do with my disability. That challenge of my family's controlling characteristics was always hard to accept because I have always felt the relationship of my family didn't share the importance of inclusion for people like myself with a disability. I never felt I had full access to opportunities while also being treated with dignity and respect, knowing how hard it was for me back then when I struggled with my education and felt socially excluded. I felt so alone that my own insecurities came out, and no one in my family or outside of my family could help me. I felt my disability was rare since no one knew about it, and where individuals like myself were included in society but on unfavorable terms. I am now actively engaged, where I share how I feel with everyone that I am around, and it helps when my surroundings show a positive vibe. I enjoy being around others who share their lives with me, whether it's professional or personal, especially people who make a difference. I like to have equal access as an individual with a disability where I don't have barriers to prevent me from participating fully in society, such as my physical accessibility issues or negative attitude, especially being in a wheelchair.

I remember being on vacation when people saw me and looked at me differently because there was no one who had a wheelchair. I also saw there was no access for wheelchairs to get around, and I was so embarrassed by how self-conscious I felt in the short term. I feel the same way when I feel awkward doing things near/with my family where I can't do the same things that I used to do as I am reminded by them, and I feel scared of being judged by them. I feel when I can't get around that much physically due to my physical disability being in a wheelchair; it affects me not doing things around my sons that much in getting around, and I feel limited being in my house alone. I wish I could go back in time and say, "Hey, look at me and see what I can do to get to know me better." I have always felt I have abilities. It just hits home deeper when my sons do things and talk to my siblings about how I can be helped. I do have to accept that my sons have different views and make up their own minds by the choices they make on my behalf.

I have to accept that my siblings and my sons use conditional love as a tool that involves expressing affection or approval based on specific behaviors or accomplishments rather than simply for who I am. I always thought unconditional love made the heart go fonder, and the bond got stronger. I also thought unconditional love offers affection without conditions and expectations, which can lead to a stronger emotional connection and a more resilient relationship. I have always been outgoing and very relatable, maybe to a fault. I am very fortunate that I am very resilient and have a deeper affection by surrounding myself with positive people who share their stories with me.

I am very active in radio broadcasting and the entertainment business. I enjoy it so much when I share my history of the past and current with radio personalities and entertainers from actors, directors, and producers who are all in the East Bay, where they come to the Orinda Theatre, where I volunteer. This is why my friend Derek Zemrak has always been very helpful to me in being involved and helping me become a productive filmmaker with all the blood, sweat, and tears that we've been through together, figuratively speaking. We both share stories from one producer to another.

We both were former Executive Producers in the film industry. Derek has done more movies than I have. I just enjoy being around him, and he has shown me the ropes and has been my mentor and friend for more than sixteen years.

I remember that, as a teenager from the late 70s through the mid-80s, I liked to engage with my parents because I had a big family, and it felt great that we had great times together. We were very active on various holidays and vacations by traveling to Europe and living in the Middle East. We often went to weddings, bars, and bat mitzvahs. I will say back to the day when I grew up in the late 70s and early 80s, I never talked back to my parents, knowing how disappointed I was internally. I just didn't show it externally because my parents were very matter-of-fact, and they didn't express their emotions because of their actions in making us happy at that moment. I never even showed my parents up or showed partiality because that's not me.

Longing For A Breakthrough

I felt that growing up as a teenager in the late 70s, I felt self-reliant because my parents never expressed their expectations for a child like me who was born with a disability. I didn't feel special or any type of inclusion because I just wanted them to acknowledge my potential, needs, and the unique challenges and joys with them.

I just wanted my relationship with my siblings to be a good one. Unfortunately, as time passed, that potentially led to neglect, in my opinion, resentments or a lack of understanding regarding social exclusion. My parents didn't set expectations and might fail to recognize that a child with a disability like myself may experience unique challenges, such as feeling overshadowed, burdened, or struggling with my own emotions. I didn't know back then if their expectations were realistic or unrealistic because they always discussed things without me and my siblings while we were all playing outside on our patio or trying to keep busy.

Conversely, my parents unconsciously, more likely consciously, placed undue pressure on me to make up for what their sibling with a disability did and did not do, leading to resentment and a feeling of being super-sibling. I wish I could say there is a lack of understanding, but without acknowledging the impact of the disability on my relationship, my parents didn't provide the support, understanding, and guidance for me to navigate my unique experience. It definitely impacted my sibling relationships. In becoming more aware of growing up with a disability, I grew up faster than kids in other families, as my mom points out to me at times. I tend to set unrealistically high expectations for myself because I have always made my feelings known. I always helped my parents and my siblings to know how to provide for me.

Jonathan Winchell

Down the road, when things happen to me, I have always learned, both short-term and long-term, how to be self-reliant. It is also important that both of my parents did not speak to me about my disability, only to each other regarding how hard it was for me because they have always done things for me and not with me so I can participate or be involved somehow so I can express myself. I know how proud my parents are of me and the rest of my siblings at the same time. I just needed attention at a time when my education wasn't as good as my siblings, and it showed. It was then that I realized when I read a quote to my dad regarding my book report that I never thought it would resonate with him, and it did. The quote that I told my dad about my book report was, *No Man is an Island*, and not only did it stop him while he was on his computer, but his response to me was I am doing the best I can. I never thought about how my words caused him to reflect on how I felt at that moment. I always had a challenge in reading because my disability wasn't good. It was below par. I do enjoy reading when it relates to self-help. I like books when it has to do with helping myself and others. I like to expand my knowledge. However, my style of reading and the way I speak to people, especially behind the words, helps me bring my ego and my emotions out. It helps me reinforce what I know so I can relate more on a personal level.

I don't get that emotion or that feeling from my family because they keep their ego to themselves, which translates to resentment and, more to the point, they are very controlling. I know my family is not patient with me due to my disability, and not what I can do as a functional adult. As a functional adult with my normal cells taking over, the struggle that I have is trying to find a healthy dose of self-belief and ambition, often associated with my ego. I know that is a powerful motivator for me to overcome my challenges and persevere through my writing process. I grew up learning to read and write through my eyes and not so much learning from teachers, which is the most traditional way of learning. I say that because my education had so many challenges in being born with Mosaic Down syndrome. I feel that being born with an intellectual disability affects my ability to learn new information, communicate, cope, and effectively solve my problems on my own, especially my education and social interactions. I know having an intellectual disability creates stress and vulnerability for both me and the support network around me. I experience problems with my abilities that make me feel confused, frustrated, and frightened. It has affected my short-term memory loss, and I find it difficult to remember certain conversations and recent events. I have a tendency to repeat stories and ask the same question over and over again.

I like focusing on new experiences by staying relevant without asking the same question. I always thought that would impress and make my family proud of me. I learned a few things on my own and observed my parents, especially growing up. I realized in my teenage years and adulthood that time was passing me up. I learned my time is all I have. I had a vision that the only way to have cohesiveness was to move on and accept that my coping abilities as a disabled individual had an impact on how my parents interacted with me, where they had their own misconceptions, which I had no control over. I wish I knew more about why inclusion is so important to me, especially since I was born with a rare disability. I believe had inclusion been involved in my teenage life, things would have been different, and it would have made my family understand my disability and relationship better. No family is perfect, and I enjoyed the time when my parents had an interest in me, even though it was at that moment in my teenage years. It is fortunate that my parents had given me tennis instructors and a former bodybuilder who taught me to do weights in my family home. It was a good experience. I learned different types of skills. It helped me a lot. I learned how to do weightlifting because I learned from an ex-professional bodybuilder who owned a company that had weights for both barbells and dumbbells that were brought to my family house.

It was a nice home gym at a time when I was very motivated and disciplined. It is unfortunate I had to learn the hard way that I had to do things on my own in following up physically and mentally to keep up with my health. In keeping up with my health, I had a lot of expectations about which muscles to work on because I learned in middle school about the muscles that I wanted to focus on. I shared my physical skills with my family. It was just unfortunate my parents had no expectations of what I could achieve because of my disability. I know, looking back, that my family thought of me as having a disability, that I am unable to do the things that able-bodied people do. I do know my disability shows great determination and dependability. I have learned my skills in tennis and in weight training, that it takes a combination of both physical and mental skills. I had physical skills like agility, balance, and eye-hand coordination, as well as mental skills such as focus, resilience, and strategic thinking. I never thought I had that because there was no reinforcement or support for what I could achieve. I never knew that when I went out for baseball, I had to develop a different type of skill that involved more power with a focus on hitting the ball hard, and that included my fielding, where I could throw far. I wouldn't say I never had a good instructor; it was because my parents didn't know any former athletes who could have trained me like I did in tennis and weight training.

I went out for football, but unfortunately, that type of skill was more strenuous, with no uniform, and time passed me up. I learned more about

Longing For A Breakthrough

baseball and hockey from my friends Ray Krause and Len Shapiro. That's when I learned a lot about statistics in baseball and went to a lot of hockey games. I first went to see NHL games with my friend Ray, who had season tickets in the mid-1990s, while watching the San Jose Sharks Sharks. That is how I have kept busy with my mental health and maintaining my passion through sports. I also went to see a lot of hockey games, such as the ECHL, by watching the Stockton Thunder and the AHL Stockton Heat, both up in Stockton, with my friend Len Shapiro. I was very active in sports, and it helped me in learning how the minor league worked and also about statistics. I also had season tickets to watch the San Francisco Giants in 2000. Sports have always helped me not just physically but also in managing my stress so I won't show my emotions. In fact, it helps me sometimes to be around my family. Any type of physical or mental activity that affects me shows my negative emotions, and sometimes, I bring it out to my family, and that's when I am unhappy. To me, that is a rare occurrence because I am very outgoing and happy. Unfortunately, it doesn't translate to good family interactions and a cohesive structure in the home being born with a disability.

I grew up in a family where they were all matter-of-fact due to their controlling characteristics, and I limit myself to being around them. I don't want my frustrations to slip out and take things personally. I feel good about myself physically and mentally by being prepared for how my day is going. I do get silly at times because I like to make people laugh. I feel good when I am around others because I like being around people from whom I can bounce ideas, and hopefully, others will feel the same way I do. I am very comfortable where I can hold my own in conversations on how to maintain a good relationship by talking to random people and getting to know them. I am pretty good at interacting with others by communicating and reaching out, especially where it helps me improve my social skills. I know it helps my character and confidence when I care and connect with others, whereas I never felt that way with my own family because, with them, I am always fighting with my patience. I have struggled with my learning disabilities that impacted my daily life, which affected my ability to learn, communicate, and perform daily activities, leading to difficulties in areas like school, work, and social interactions.

I now understand that my Mosaic Down syndrome is a neurological disorder that affects my brain development and function, which can lead to my developmental delays and intellectual disabilities. With all that said, I am an individual who finds the strength to endure overwhelming obstacles in a family-type setting. I had an uncontrolled personality type when I was younger, and it appeared erratic or expressively expressive, especially being overcontrolled by family members who were distant and overly reserved, especially after my dad passed away. I felt like dealing with my behavior was getting better when I didn't show my emotions in public display, like no temper tantrums and no impulsive behaviors. An uncontrolled child like me frequently had difficulty exercising self-control and displaying emotional gestures or mild aggressive behavior, to say the least.

Being a parent, I am aware of how hard it was to help my two boys with their education, and it reflected in how I communicated. It was a struggle to be self-reliant in my daily life due to my disability. I also have problems with my limited mobility issues that impact certain physical activities around my house and outside. I can still do dishes, and I can do my own laundry. I just take a while to get things done, as I am reminded.

I am involved in volunteering at the California Historical Radio Society in Alameda, California, where I have five years of experience in broadcasting. I enjoy communicating with my fellow broadcasters when I am in Alameda when there are radio events. I used to volunteer as a photographer for the Bay Area Radio Hall of Fame induction events for ten years.

I volunteer now where there's still work to be done. I personally like talking about the history of radio broadcasting from 1900 through the 1920s, which all started in Alameda, California, at the California Historical Radio Society. I like collecting all broadcasting and media ephemera. That means saving items like old radio stations, newspaper clippings related to media, promotional materials from media outlets, and other materials related to broadcasting.

I also volunteer for the Orinda Theatre, where I run the box office. I meet and greet others at the front door, and I direct them to what theatre they have to watch the movie they are seeing. I also run the concession stands when needed. I also enjoy physical activities such as cleaning the lobby at the Orinda Theatre in Orinda, California. I prefer to work in the box office so I can be around the public, which I have done for a while. I am also a volunteer at the Orinda Historical Society. I am a photographer, and I take pictures of everything about Orinda, everything from 1941 to the time when the Orinda Theatre was built. It was also where the first movie came to the Orinda Theatre; the title of the movie was *Texas*, starring William Holden, Glenn Ford, and Claire Trevor from December 27th, 1941.

So, my goal is to volunteer from one day to seven days a week and expand my horizons so I can work on various projects. I love helping out my community from the city of Alameda and Orinda.

Jonathan Winchell

I do like to get around and not stay in my house for a period of time because I get very restless trying to figure out what I need to do on a day-to-day basis. One of the main reasons for me not getting out that much is due to the physical limitations that limit me in walking, and it is a strain on my lower back due to a pinched nerve that makes it hard to move around. I rest more frequently, whether I am on my recliner or in bed, and it makes it easier. I do get out of the house by being around my friends with whom I have a connection and interest. I just enjoy being around people who are outgoing and talk about their hobbies, are sports-oriented, and interested in what I do by volunteering my services to various organizations. I am trying to find a way to volunteer on a permanent basis, which makes me happy. I have to say that being semi-retired is not easy, especially when I was working full-time in a family business, where I took an active role from 1985 through 2015. I am still actively involved in keeping my mental faculties ahead of the game, which means I try to stay active.

I enjoy the experience of being a volunteer in the long run so I can be successful in various activities mentally and physically. I like sharing what I do day by day. I would like to share with my family if they actually show an interest in what I have to say. I do know that my family only wants to see me and not hear from me. I published my first book in 2022, and as I am working on my second manuscript, I have collaborated with my family by getting them involved. I have not received any feedback on how I can improve my writing. I focus on a lot of editing because I spend an excessive amount of time trying to get things right and find situations without order and structure challenging. I always notice what is out of line and feel compelled to fix it, especially with my relationship and family dynamics. In conclusion, I always feel I must be in control of my impulses.

Chapter 12: My Future Plans

I see a future where I can provide funding for cities in the Bay Area or in the East Bay that need improvement in thriving locations and new development or programs to improve the quality of life. I have done twenty years of funding for non-profit organizations that are 501 (C3). I did research in my hometown of Lafayette, California, where I was born in the mid-60s. It was a thriving city in the 1950s. I even remember being an underwriter for the entire LASF program and not only for my son's education; it was for the whole community at a time when the Lafayette Arts Science Foundation all came together. I would like to be a director or an executive director in the future, where I can make a big difference not just in my community but in other communities as well. I have given my time, effort, and resources to help out with cities in the Bay Area and outside of the Bay Area.

I find it very comforting, and I would like to create a support group that supports inclusion when it regards my disability and other disabilities by sharing with others how it is important to me. I have grown and evolved, and how it reflects my experiences and the choices I have made. I get really emotional about my disability because I have strong feelings and empathy for myself and others around me.

I would consider myself an empath because I have strong emotions when I see, read, or hear about people less fortunate than me. I used to look at myself as being developmentally challenged due to my rare disability and how it affected the lack of my ability to interact with others and with my family. It has now evolved for the better, where my quality of life has improved, and I have more friends and more social activities. I also know there are times in the present when my mother and my siblings look at me differently after my dad passed away, especially at family functions, which is not as much as it used to be when my dad was alive. That's all they see about me and want to talk about when we get together. I have shared my experiences and choices I make about my health and well-being with my family on how hard it is for me to cope with in regards to my disability, past and present. I still need help with loose ends that I still have to deal with. I just don't want to reflect too much and overthink about how I can do better when I am around my family. I like to stick with the present so I can stay relevant. I do know how inclusion will help me with my relationship with my mother and my siblings. I still have unresolved issues that I need to effectively resolve and understand how I need to be respected. I do need to feel included, so inclusion will help me feel emotional satisfaction, especially when I feel comfortable around my family.

I do feel for people who don't know me or what my disability is, especially those who are suffering from disabilities like Mosaic Down syndrome, so much so that they need a support group. I would like to be an advocate for them. I am very sensitive when it has to do with being excluded due to my disability, especially when my family is overprotective of me. I do find it interesting that when my dad was alive and was the patriarch of the family, all of these personal conflicts that have been going on from 2016 until now have never existed before. There has definitely been more of a role in my family taking care of me due to my disability, which, in my mind, I have done more to take care of myself now than I did when my parents took care of me way before my dad passed away. I have definitely observed that there are more conflicts, and it is important to note that, being in a family business for over thirty years, I decided to move on to show my independence, and that is how I worked things out. I do like it when making a difference; it shows that my relationship with my family is important and for the better. That is where the cracks fall, where I express my thoughts and feelings, and anytime my position is different from theirs, they avoid any type of confrontation, and they don't share their differences with me when they arise. I feel it is okay to express one's ego. It lets everyone know where I stand and how I feel, and it can turn out positively. I never liked the feeling of holding grudges or resentment.

I enjoy being around people who are positive and hearing how I can improve. I do hear a lot of stories where people outside of my family appreciate me and enjoy being around me. I like to be needed, especially when I volunteer and am around people who are community-oriented. I see a lot of closures of various businesses, and it makes me want to do more volunteer work. It really means a lot to me. I like to see myself directly communicating with others and having face-to-face conversations by locally engaging myself full-time. I enjoy volunteering at the Orinda Theatre, where I provide my services at the box office. I also like sharing my first book online, titled *Being Different Than My Family*. It explains more about who I am and how I evolved through hard times in being born with Mosaic Down syndrome. I would like to play an active role in my community on a daily basis where I can embrace future challenges from the ground up. I hope it can lead to future endeavors. I am an extrovert, and I can handle all the stresses of the outside world. It has caused me in a positive way to effectively use my different forms of communication, but the process of bringing them to fruition has a necessary, sometimes overlooked step where I felt a mix of pure relief and joy, and I sometimes minimize my feelings and the ability to walk away. I don't like the feeling when I walk away from my work and family.

Jonathan Winchell

It just takes me a while to get back on track. I like taking time for myself, which may take me minutes, hours, and days to realize that I just like the thrill of looking at my life differently with my fresh eyes wide open. I do like to see the errors of my ways where I don't see or hear them with others who don't see the errors of their ways. I have realized that my overall tone and structure take longer, so I can effectively communicate better when I send emails, text to others, or a story that I want to tell and live a normal day-to-day life. Now, I understand that things are not as simple as being right or wrong.

www.ingramcontent.com/pod-product-compliance
Lightning Source LLC
Chambersburg PA
CBHW051606010526
44119CB00056B/802